W9-CEZ-590

PURCHASING ORGANIZATIONAL RELATIONSHIPS

by

Harold E. Fearon

Center for Advanced Purchasing Studies/
National Association of Purchasing Management, Inc.

PURCHASING ORGANIZATIONAL RELATIONSHIPS

by

Harold E. Fearon, Ph.D., C.P.M.
Director
Center for Advanced Purchasing Studies

ACKNOWLEDGMENTS •

THE CENTER FOR ADVANCED PURCHASING STUDIES wishes to thank the purchasing executives in the 297 organizations who provided the data on their organizations to provide the basis for this study.

The work of Chiang-nan Chao in the coding of the data and preparation of the tables was key to the prompt completion of the overall study. Carol Ketchum assisted in preparation of the final manuscript.

Finally, four purchasing executives/academics served on the ad-hoc industry/research advisory committee for this study. Their comments and review of the draft manuscript helped strengthen the analysis of the data. Special thanks is due to:

1. John Cologna, General Electric Company
2. Montague E. Cooper, Chevron U.S.A., Inc.
3. George A. Harris, TRW, Inc.
4. Michael G. Kolchin, Lehigh University

Of course, complete responsibility for the final study results rests with the director of this research project.

ISBN   0-945968-00-0

LCCN : 88-148548

CONTENTS •

TABLES •

SUMMARY OF SURVEY DATA •

THIS REPORT IS BASED ON DATA COLLECTED in April, 1987 from 297 U.S. organizations in 23 industry groups. Of the 297 organizations, 84 (28%) had 1986 sales of less than $500 million; 45 (15%) had sales of $.5 to 1 billion; 110 (37%) were in the $1.1 to 5 billion sales category; 31 (10%) in the $5.1 to 10 billion sales category; and 27 (9%) had 1986 sales of over $10 billion.

The study found that:

1. The average size of the professional purchasing staff was 118. This ranged from an average of only 14 persons in the organizations in the smallest size category to 366 and 485 persons in the two largest size categories.

2. The majority of the organizations (59%) were organized on a centralized/ decentralized basis, in which some purchasing is done at the corporate headquarters as well as at major operating divisions/ plants. Twenty-eight percent had a centralized function in which all or almost all purchasing is done at one central location. Only 13% were decentralized, in which purchasing was done on a division/plant basis.

3. The purchasing function reports to the president in 16% of the organizations and to the executive vice president in 18%. The most-common reporting relationship is to a manufacturing/production/operations vice president (24%). Other reporting relationships are to an administrative vice president (13%), materials management vice president (8%), financial vice president (7%), and engineering vice president (1%). Twelve percent report elsewhere in the organization.

4. Scrap/surplus disposal reports to purchasing in 57% of the organizations, inbound traffic in 41%, inventory control in 37%, warehousing or stores in 34%, outbound traffic in 32%, receiving in 26%, and incoming inspection in 16%.

5. The three functions which most-commonly have been newly assigned to purchasing since 1980 were personnel travel, traffic/transportation, and countertrade/offset planning/execution.

6. Purchasing has assumed an increased role or responsibility since 1980 in strategic planning, providing economic forecasts/indicators, capital equipment buys, product development, new product evaluation, and traffic/transportation.

7. The materials management concept, in which at least three of the following functions: purchasing, inventory, production scheduling and control, inbound traffic, warehousing and stores, and incoming quality control report to a single responsible individual was used by 70% of the organizations.

8. The function which most frequently reports to the materials manager is inventory, followed closely by purchasing, and warehousing and stores.

9. The chief purchasing officer typically:
   a. carries the title of director of purchasing (38%). The next most-used titles are vice president of purchasing (23%) and manager of purchasing (18%)
   b. is just under 50 years of age
   c. holds a bachelor's degree (94%); 39% hold an advanced degree
   d. did his or her bachelor's degree work in business
   e. has been in his or her position for 6 years
   f. has been with his or her employer for 18 years
   g. has a total of 17 years of experience in purchasing and 4 years in operations/production.

5

IMPLICATIONS OF THE SURVEY DATA •

While a survey research study of this type does not provide definitive proof of cause and effect, and often raises as many questions as it provides answers, it does provide an indication of developing trends. While interpretations of the data will differ, the following ten developments should be considered by executives in charge of various purchasing activities and by academics and researchers concerned with further development of purchasing and people performing the functions:

1. The average professional staff size of 118 is surprisingly large; for the total of 297 organizations, that represents a total of over 35,000 professional purchasing personnel. An extrapolation of these data to the total *Fortune* 1,000 list would indicate that there are well over 100,000 professional purchasing personnel in this group of very large organizations.

The numbers from this 1987 CAPS study are substantially larger than the average of 20 persons shown in the previous 1960 American Management Association study. While the two studies are not exactly comparable, it does seem to indicate that the number of professional purchasing personnel in the typical large organization has increased over the past 25 years.

2. The continuum of types of organizations for purchasing (from centralized to decentralized) is very wide. Our study placed all 296 responding firms at one of only three points—centralized, centralized/decentralized, or decentralized. However, it seems clear that most organizations try to get the best of all possible worlds, by making a mix between centralization *and* decentralization.

3. The most-common reporting relationship has the purchasing function reporting to the vice president of manufacturing/operations/production. This implies that the importance of the purchasing function to the production process still remains paramount. However, top-level status of the purchasing function is shown by the fact that in 34% of the organizations the purchasing function reports to either the president or executive vice president.

4. In spite of the discussions in the U.S. and particularly in Europe about the wisdom of organizing on a logistics basis, with all materials flow functions (both incoming and outgoing) reporting to a logistics manager, it appears to be little used in actual practice. Purchasing reports to a logistics manager in less than 1% of the organizations.

5. The purchasing function has assumed a wide functional span; the inbound traffic activity is a purchasing responsiblity in 41% of the organizations, and inventory control reports to purchasing in 37% of the organizations. Incoming inspection, which conventional wisdom says must be separated from purchasing to assure proper checks and balances, is a purchasing responsibility in 16% of the organizations. This broader functional responsibility for purchasing argues that the purchasing executive needs an educational and experience background that encompasses much more than only the traditional purchasing function.

6. With transport deregulation (which began in 1977) purchasing has assumed a new responsibility in many organizations for buying personnel travel services for company employees and for freight services. An increased number of organizations has placed a new responsibility for countertrade/offset planning/execution on purchasing. In the past, this often was thought to be solely a marketing activity. This implies that the scope of the purchasing function has been expanded in many organizations to encompass the purchase of services and the making

of countertrade purchases in direct support of the marketing activity.

7. The increased role of purchasing in strategic planning, providing economic forecasts, capital equipment buys, and product development recognizes the movement to a top-level corporate support position, as opposed to only a material-acquisition-and-flow interest. This implies that the people in purchasing must have broader abilities and an understanding of the overall mission and functioning of the organization.

8. Materials management appears to be the predominant method of organizing the materials acquisition and flow activities. Purchasing people must develop a new understanding of the various materials functions if the improved coordination, communication, and control benefits of materials management are to be realized.

9. The head of the purchasing function now is seldom considered to be only an agent of the organization. Instead, the chief purchasing officer now typically carries a title denoting director or vice president status and responsibility. A college degree, normally in business, seems to be a prerequisite to the top position in purchasing, and an advanced degree seems now to be a requirement for the top position in many organizations.

10. While a more-varied experience background seems to be called for on the part of the chief purchasing officer, due to the broader role of purchasing in today's organizations, in most instances his or her background has been primarily in purchasing. This indicates that changes must take place in many organization's job rotation planning if their personnel are to obtain the broader functional background needed to meet the demands of tomorrow.

DESIGN OF THIS STUDY •

THE CENTER FOR ADVANCED PURCHASING STUDIES (CAPS) did this research on purchasing organizational relationships (its first research project since CAPS was organized in November, 1986), with three objectives:

1. To provide business people and academics with current, accurate information on various facets of purchasing organization and operation. Managers can compare their organizational patterns and operations with those of other organizations. This can be done in total, by industry groups, or by organizational size (measured by 1986 sales dollars).

2. To update data on purchasing organizational relationships, so that when the question, "How is purchasing organized?" is posed, current information can be supplied. Thus, these new CAPS data reflect the changes which have taken place over the past several years.

3. To "baseline" where purchasing now is organizationally. CAPS plans to update these data periodically, to highlight changes which occur.

The Sample: To obtain the data, a 5-page questionnaire was prepared and sent in April, 1987 to 562 organizations, with a cover letter and stamped return envelope. The organizations were selected from the *Fortune* 1000 list, plus some smaller firms and selected quasi-government (nonprofit research) organizations.

Questionnaires were sent *only* to organizations in which the chief purchasing executive could be identified by name and title, through one of the published directories. The intent was to obtain at least 200 usable responses.

Of the 562 questionnaires mailed, 22 were either returned by the post office as undeliverable (typically because the individual no longer was at that address) or because the address had changed. Three organizations responded that company policy precluded completion of the questionnaire. Thus, the potential survey group was 540 organizations.

A total of 297 usable responses was received, a 55% response rate. Because of the response percentage, no follow-up mailing or telephone contacts to non-respondees was made. This was an unusually high response to a questionnaire survey and lends credibility to the resultant data and analysis.

Table 1 presents the number of usable responses received, broken down by the 23 industry groups and by size of organization (by 1986 sales revenue categories). Industry group 6, "Government/Nonprofit" consists of technical research and development organizations, in which the 1986 "billing for services provided" is the equivalent of sales income. No responses were received from the Leather and Leather Products industry group.

The largest number of responses was in industry group 36, Electric, Electronic Equipment (40 companies); 20, Food and Beverage and 28, Chemicals (32 companies each) and 29, Petroleum and Coal (22 companies). The lowest response total was in 5, Retail/Trade/Distribution, with only 2 responding firms. Three of the industry groups, 23, Apparel; 24, Lumber and Wood; and 25, Furniture and Fixtures, each had only 3 responses. This reduces confidence in the data analysis for those 4 industry groups. It is recognized that a given firm may have divisions in more than one industry, and that assigning a firm to its primary industry group may have resulted in some less-than-totally-accurate analysis.

On a sales basis, the 297 organizations were well distributed. The largest category was the 110 organizations in the $1.1 to 5 billion category; the lowest was 27 in the over

$10 billion sales category. An organization often includes a number of different divisions.

The respondents to the survey were promised complete anonymity. No individual organizations can be identified; only aggregate data are presented.

All data responses were loaded into a data base on a mini computer and the tables for analysis were prepared through a relatively-simple computer program. Since the data all are on the computer data base, many additional cross comparisons, in addition to those presented in the body of the study, could be made. However, the need to keep the report relatively short required that the presentation of data be limited to three analytical formats: by industry group, by organization size, and by each of the 23 specific industries. The major topics on which data were collected were:

1. Size of professional staffs
2. Organization of the purchasing function
3. To whom purchasing reports
4. Functions which report to purchasing
5. Activity areas newly assigned to purchasing
6. Activity areas in which purchasing has assumed an increased role or responsibility
7. Use of the materials management concept
8. The functions included in materials management
9. The chief purchasing officer (CPO): title, age, education, years in present position, years with present employer, and years experience in various functional areas.

No salary information was collected, for two reasons: (1) that information is readily available from a number of sources and normally is updated annually, and (2) such information is sensitive in many organizations; requesting it probably would have reduced the response rate.

The data are analyzed and presented in three major groupings:

1. By the 23 industry groups, the combined 20 groups in manufacturing, and in total.
2. By organizational size, broken down into 5 dollar categories (1986 sales revenues).
3. By each of the individual 23 industry groupings, for ease of analysis when one wishes to see the organizational pattern for a specific industry.

PURCHASING ORGANIZATIONAL RELATIONSHIPS •

INCREASED INTEREST IN and attention to the purchasing function has been evident during the decade of the 1980s. It has evolved through several stages:

1. The perception, during the early third of the century, that it primarily is a clerical-type activity,
2. The shortage-induced attention of World War II (1939-1945),
3. The return-on-assets measurement influence during the 1950s and 60s,
4. The supply crises of the early 1970s, which saw severe world-wide material shortages and rapidly-escalating prices,[1] and
5. The need to source globally during the 1980s to achieve the quality and cost levels required to compete with Far East manufacturers in the automotive and electronics industries.

Purchasing now is looked at by many organizations as one of the key factors in the race for increased productivity and competitiveness. Recently *The Kiplinger Washington Letter* commented that the role of the purchasing manager is changing, as it moves from a clerical-type task to a top-management emphasis, because of its potential contributions in cost control, global sourcing, and just-in-time purchasing systems. It further observed that purchasing now is regarded as one of the paths to the CEO's suite.[2]

It now is well recognized that changes have taken place in the purchasing function and the way it is performed. The people in purchasing, the organizational level of purchasing, reporting relationships, and functions performed are not the same as they were a decade or so ago. However, empirical data on the organizational relationships of purchasing have not kept pace with the changes taking place. One of the most-asked questions posed to the National Association of Purchasing Management Information Center over the past several years is, "How do firms organize to perform the purchasing function?" The comparison between how a given company organizes and how a large group of firms is organized often can provide useful insights to the manager. The primary sources of empirical data available on purchasing organizational relationships are:

1. *Aljian's Purchasing Handbook*, Fourth edition, 1982. In section 2, "The Purchasing Organization," a figure is given on "Who's purchasing's immediate boss," taken from *Purchasing* magazine. This identical figure appears also in the third edition and is identified as coming from the December 9, 1971 *Purchasing* magazine, i.e., it now is over 15 years old.

A table in the fourth edition presents statistics on "To Whom Purchasing Reports, Based on Company Size." The text referring to this table states that the data presented "are based on an earlier research study of 350 respondents made for this handbook." A comparison of the second (1966), third (1973), and fourth (1982) editions indicates that the statistics for this table are the same. The reference to the table in the second edition shows that the survey was conducted in 1963, i.e., the data are 25 years old. Thus they probably do not fairly represent the changes that have occurred and the current organizational situation.[3]

2. *Purchasing Department Organization and Authority*, 1960. This study was based on data collected by the American Management Association through a questionnaire sent to 750 companies selected at random from *Poor's Register of Directors and Executives*. Usable responses were received from 147 companies (a 19 percent response rate). Based on the data supplied by the company respondents, information was presented on "1. The Purchasing Personnel Ratio, 2. The

Purchasing Operating Expense Ratio, 3. To Centralize or to Decentralize?, 4. Purchasing Department Authority, 5. Departmental Status and Reporting Relationships, and 6. The Purchasing Manual: Its Uses and Content."[4] But these data now also are over 25 years old.

SIZE OF PROFESSIONAL STAFFS

It was expected that, with few exceptions, the numbers of professional purchasing personnel would be relatively small, since a large number of purchase requirements can be handled by relatively-few personnel. The 1960 American Management Association study had found (for the 143 total firms which responded) the average number of purchasing personnel per firm was slightly under 20. This number was consistent for both the 127 firms in manufacturing and the 16 non-manufacturing firms. This AMA study further found, as would be expected, that the number of personnel increased with organization size as measured by gross income, i.e.,[5]

Under $5 million	4	personnel	(average)
$5 to 25 million	9	"	"
$25 to 100 million	24	"	"
Over $100 million	75	"	"

The CAPS study focused heavily on large to very-large organizations, and of the 290 organizations supplying personnel data, 208 (72%) had 1986 sales of $500 million or more. The data are company-level, rather than division-level, information. As Table 2 shows, the average number of professional purchasing personnel was substantially greater in the larger organizations, i.e.,

Under $500 million	14	professionals	(average)
$500 million to 1 billion	42	"	"
$1.1 to 5 billion	71	"	"
$5.1 to 10 billion	366	"	"
Over $10 billion	485	"	"

In the under $500 million sales category, of the 82 responding organizations 79, or 96%, employed 25 or fewer professionals. Only one organization in the $5.1 to 10 billion category, and none in the over $10 billion category employed 25 or fewer professionals. Only one organization in the two smallest size categories (126 total organiza-

tions responding) employed 251 or more employees. However, 26 of the 56 organizations (46%) in the two largest size categories employed 251 or more purchasing professionals. Five of these organizations had over 1,000 purchasing professionals on their payroll.

Table 3 shows the number of professional purchasing personnel by the 23 industry categories. The 256 firms in the manufacturing sector had an average of 126 purchasing professionals. The 29 firms in the service sector employed an average of 64 purchasing professionals. In descending order, the average number of employees were:

Aerospace	421	professionals	(average)
Transportation Equipment	269	"	"
Electric, Electronic Equipment	233	"	"
Fabricated Metal Products	138	"	"
Chemicals	124	"	"
Petroleum and Coal	97	"	"
Stone, Clay, Glass	70	"	"
Service	64	"	"
Miscellaneous Manufacturing	54	"	"
Paper	47	"	"
Machinery, except Electrical	43	"	"
Food and Beverage	42	"	"
Rubber and Plastics	41	"	"
Primary Metals	40	"	"
Government-nonprofit	36	"	"
Instruments, Related Products	34	"	"
Tobacco Products	32	"	"
Furniture and Fixtures	29	"	"
Textile Mill Product	28	"	"
Printing and Publishing	18	"	"
Lumber and Wood	14	"	"
Apparel	13	"	"
Retail/Trade/Distribution	12	"	"

Thus, there is a great deal of difference in the sizes of professional purchasing staffs, from the relatively-small sizes in Retail/Trade/Distribution; Apparel; Lumber and Wood; Printing and Publishing; and Textile Mill Product, to the staffs which are from 8 to 35 times greater in Aerospace; Transportation Equipment; and Electric, Electronic Equipment. The industries with the smaller staffs tend to be those which produce simple or limited product lines. The industries with the larger-size staffs produce complex products, requiring purchasing inputs from literally thousands of vendors from around the world.

ORGANIZATION OF THE PURCHASING FUNCTION

It appears that the majority of the organizations have reached a compromise to the question of centralization versus decentralization, as shown by the overall responses to the question of how they are organized, i.e.,

Centralized	28% of the organizations
Centralized/Decentralized	59% " " "
Decentralized	13% " " "

Table 4 presents the data by company size. Obviously, there is a wide continuum of possible organizational relationships, from totally centralized to totally decentralized, and a particular organization might be anywhere on that spectrum. The centralized form of organization, in which all or almost all purchasing is done at one central location for the entire firm, appears a less-used organizational arrangement as organizations grow in total size, e.g., 44% of organizations in the smallest size category use this form of organization, but this declines steadily and is used by only 15% of the organizations in the largest category.

The percent of organizations with a decentralized organization structure, in which purchasing is done on a division/plant basis, is at the 11 to 14% level in all five size categories. These relatively-low percents probably are due to the reality that only with some form of centralized purchasing can an organization achieve the real potential of volume buying.

Centralized/decentralized purchasing, in which some purchasing is done at the corporate headquarters and purchasing also is done centrally at major operating divisions/plants, appears to be more common as organizations grow larger. Only 42% of the organizations in the smallest size category use this form, but it becomes more common with the larger organizations. Seventy-four percent of the organizations in the two largest size categories are organized in this manner. Evidently this form of organization allows them to combine the advantages of having purchasing decisions made at the location of the requirements, with the advantages of volume buying which come from handling certain requirements on a centralized (aggregate) basis.

Centralized/decentralized purchasing by industry group:

Table 5 presents the organizational data by industry group.

The comparison of the 20 groups in the manufacturing sector and the service sector shows:

	Manufacturing (262 firms)	Service (28 firms)
Centralized	26%	36%
Centralized/Decentralized	60%	61%
Decentralized	14%	4%
	100%	101%

In only three of the industry groups were over one-third of the firms organized on a decentralized basis: Fabricated Metals Products (56%), Miscellaneous Manufacturing (43%), and Machinery, except Electrical (36%). The centralized/decentralized mode was the arrangement most used by the majority of the industry groups. In the following groups at least half the organizations were organized on a centralized/decentralized basis:

Lumber and Wood	100%
Furniture and Fixtures	100
Chemicals	81
Stone, Clay, Glass	80
Petroleum & Coal	77
Primary Metals	73
Printing and Publishing	71
Electric, Electronic Equipment	63
Aerospace	61
Service	60
Transportation Equipment	58
Food and Beverage	53
Rubber and Plastics	50
Retail/Trade/Distribution	50

TO WHOM PURCHASING REPORTS

The reporting relationship of purchasing is important, since it is a sign of organizational status and a key to purchasing's influence within the organization. Previous studies (although the sample was not directly comparable to this CAPS study) found that:

13

A. 1960 AMA Study (147 companies):[6] Company official or committee to whom the head of the purchasing department reports:

President	29%
Executive VP	8
Vice President	7
VP-Manufacturing	4
Treasurer	3
VP & General Manager	3
General Manager	3
Other	43
	100%

B. *Purchasing Handbook*, 1963 study (survey of 350 nationally recognized leaders of the purchasing profession).[7]

To whom purchasing reports:

President	34.7%
Vice President	25.4
Executive VP	13.9
Plant Manager	5.2
General Manager	8.3
Treasurer	2.6
Miscellaneous	9.9

C. *Purchasing* magazine, 1971 study (survey of 500 purchasing managers):[8]

Who's purchasing's immediate boss?

President	26%
Manufacturing VP	22
Executive VP	13
Materials Manager	9
Procurement VP	7
Financial VP	4
Other	19

This 1987 CAPS study found that for the 291 organizations reporting these data purchasing reports to (Table 6):

President	16%
Executive VP	18
Financial VP	7
Mfg/prod/opns VP	24
Materials Management VP	8
Engineering VP	1
Administrative VP	13
Other	12
	99%

Table 6 presents the reporting relationships by company size. For the smallest size group, in 13% of the organizations purchasing reports to the president, 12% to the executive VP, and 33% to a manufacturing/production/operations VP. The organizations in the larger size categories have purchasing more commonly reporting to the president or the executive VP; in the $5.1-10 billion category,

a total of 61% report to either the president or executive VP; in the over $10 billion category, 35% report to the president or the executive VP. However, in these larger organizations, the percent reporting to the manufacturing/production/operations VP drops to only 10% and 12%. The percent reporting to the financial VP increases to 19% in the largest size category.

In only two of the 291 firms (less than 1%) did purchasing report to a logistics manager, indicating that the logistics-type organization is not commonly used in today's organizations.

Table 7 presents the reporting relationship by industry groups; those in which over 40% report to the president or the executive VP were:

	To President	To Exec. VP	Total
Fabricated Metal Products	33%	33%	66%
Rubber and Plastics	30	30	60
Food and Beverage	32	19	51
Retail/Trade/Distribution	0	50	50
Primary Metals	31	15	46
Service	24	21	45
Aerospace	18	24	42

FUNCTIONS WHICH REPORT TO PURCHASING

The specific purchasing-related activities which report to the purchasing function vary widely between different organizations. Table 8 shows the functions which report to purchasing in total and by the five size categories. In decending order, the total percentages are:

Function	Percent of organizations in which function reports to purchasing
Scrap/surplus disposal	57%
*Inbound traffic	41
Inventory control	37
Warehousing or stores	34
*Outbound traffic	32
Both inbound and outbound traffic	31
Receiving	26
Incoming inspection	16

*The 41% for inbound traffic combines the 10% for inbound traffic and the 31% for both inbound and outbound; the 32% for outbound traffic combines the 1% for outbound and the 31% for both inbound and outbound.

The logic for scrap/surplus disposal reporting to purchasing is that purchasing has knowledge of market demands and prices for scrap/surplus items and the communication channels through which information can be obtained. Performance of the inbound traffic function relates very closely to the purchasing decision on source, method of shipment, and overall cost/price paid, which accounts for the 41% which report to purchasing.

Incoming inspection is tied closely to the purchasing function, however in the past many organizations felt that it should be separated from purchasing so that the pressure to have items in house on a certain date would not cause a compromise on quality standards. Yet this study shows that 16% of the organizations have incoming inspection report to purchasing, evidently assuming that the purchasing decision-makers have a total understanding of the overall organizational needs and that the risk of compromising quality standards is not a major problem.

Functions reporting to purchasing by industry groups: Table 9 shows the data by the 23 industry groups. A comparison between the manufacturing sector and the service sector shows wide diversity between five of the functions:

	Function Reports to Purchasing in:	
	Manufacturing	Service
Both inbound and out- bound traffic	29%	45%
Warehousing or stores	31	62
Inventory control	35	55
Receiving	23	52
Incoming inspection	15	28

Evidently, the purchasing activity encompasses more functional areas in the service-type organizations than in manufacturing. This implies a broader role for the purchasing managers in service-type organizations.

ACTIVITY AREAS NEWLY ASSIGNED (SINCE 1980) TO PURCHASING

One of the objectives of the CAPS study was to identify trends which are taking place in the evolution of the purchasing function. While the respondents were asked to identify "activity areas newly assigned, since 1980, to purchasing," it is recognized that a precise identification of activity areas by date probably was not possible. However, the results, in decending order, do identify the major changes which have taken place over the past seven or so years:

	Assigned, since 1980, to purchasing
Personnel travel	14%
Traffic/transportation	13
Countertrade/offset planning/execution	12
Strategic planning	9
Capital equipment buys	7
Providing economic forecasts/indicators	6
New product evaluation	4
Cash-flow planning	4
Product development	3
Commodity futures trading	3
Marketing planning	1

Table 10 presents the data by size of organization. The percentages, by activity, are largely similar by size groups, however none of the organizations in the two largest size categories were involved in Product Development, Marketing Planning, Providing Economic Forecasts/Indicators, Commodity Futures Trading, and Cash-Flow Planning. This may be because these larger organizations have full-time personnel or staffs available to concentrate on these five activities, and it is not a specific involvement area for purchasing.

Activity areas newly assigned, by industry groups: Table 11 breaks the data down by the 23 industries. The areas showing at 20% or over are:

Strategic planning: Tobacco Products (20%), Apparel (33%), Machinery, except Electrical (29%).

Traffic/transportation: Textile Mill Product (33%), Stone, Clay, Glass (60%), Primary Metals (21%), Fabricated Metal Products (33%), Machinery, except Electrical (21%),

15

Retail/Trade/Distribution (50%), and Government-nonprofit (33%).

New product evaluation: Apparel (33%), Machinery, except Electrical (29%), Retail/Trade/Distribution (50%).

Capital equipment buys: Stone, Clay, Glass (20%), Machinery, except Electrical (21%), Miscellaneous Manufacturing (21%), Retail/Trade/Distribution (50%).

Personnel travel: Tobacco Products (20%), Electric, Electronic Equipment (20%), Instruments, Related Products (40%), Retail/Trade/Distribution (50%), Government-nonprofit (33%), Service (21%).

Providing economic forecasts/indicators: Textile Mill Product (33%), Machinery, except Electrical (21%).

Commodity futures trading: Furniture and Fixtures (33%).

Countertrade/offset planning/execution: Furniture and Fixtures (33%), Stone, Clay, Glass (40%), Primary Metals (29%), Fabricated Metal Products (33%), Instruments, Related Products (20%), Aerospace (33%).

ACTIVITY AREAS IN WHICH PURCHASING HAS ASSUMED AN INCREASED ROLE OR RESPONSIBILITY (SINCE 1980)

A substantially-higher percent of the organizations indicated that purchasing had assumed an increase role/responsibility since 1980 for each of the activity areas than the percent which indicated it had been newly assigned to purchasing. Also, the top three activity areas newly assigned were different than the top three in which purchasing has assumed an increased role or responsibility. The areas in descending order were:

	An increased role/responsibility since 1980
Strategic planning	43%
Providing economic forecasts/indicators	41
Capital equipment buys	37
Product development	31
New product evaluation	26
Traffic/transportation	23
Personnel travel	16
Countertrade/offset planning/execution	15
Cash-flow planning	13
Marketing planning	9
Commodity futures trading	6

Table 12 presents the data by size of organization. Strategic planning, Providing economic forecasts/indicators, and Capital equipment buys are the areas in which organizations in all size categories have assumed greater responsibility over the past seven years. At least 20% of all the organizations indicated these areas, and the percentages were substantially larger in most of the size groups. The smaller percentages for increased role/responsibility were in the two largest size categories, and specifically for the activities of Traffic/transportation, New product evaluation, Marketing planning, Commodity futures trading, and Cash-flow planning. Conceivably this is because the larger organizations have full-time personnel assigned to these activities.

Activity areas in which purchasing has assumed an increased role/responsibility, by industry groups: Table 13 breaks the data down by the 23 industries. The activity areas showing at 50% or more are:

Strategic planning: Apparel (67%), Paper (71%), Printing and Publishing (50%), Chemicals (53%), Fabricated Metal Products (56%), Transportation Equipment (67%), Miscellaneous Manufacturing (64%), Aerospace (50%), Government-nonprofit (67%).

Product development: Apparel (67%), Furniture and Fixtures (67%), Transportation Equipment (50%), Miscellaneous Manufacturing (57%), Retail/Trade/Distribution (50%).

Traffic/transportation: Lumber and Wood (67%), Paper (50%), Instruments and Related Products (60%), Retail/Trade/Distribution (50%).

New product evaluation: Apparel (67%), Furniture and Fixtures (67%), Transportation Equipment (50%).

Capital equipment buys: Textile Mill Product (50%), Lumber and Wood (67%), Furniture and Fixtures (67%), Paper (57%), Printing and Publishing (50%), Chemicals (53%), Retail/Trade/Distribution (50%), Government-nonprofit (67%).

Personnel travel: Lumber and Wood (67%), Printing and Publishing (50%), Government-nonprofit (67%).

Providing economic forecasts/indicators: Tobacco Products (60%), Lumber and Wood (67%), Paper (86%), Printing and Publishing

16

(67%), Chemicals (50%), Rubber and Plastics (50%), Primary Metals (50%), Transportation Equipment (50%), Miscellaneous Manufacturing (50%).

Evidently the changing requirements and new opportunities of the business world of the 1980s have caused the purchasing function to take on new roles and assume additional responsibilities in areas which largely were unknown a few decades ago.

THE MATERIALS MANAGEMENT CONCEPT

While there are various definitions of what the materials management concept includes, e.g., does it go beyond the point of the introduction of materials and services into production and extend into the distribution of goods and services into the marketplace?, this study used a definition of the materials management concept as "an organization in which at least *three* of the following functions—purchasing, inventory, production scheduling and control, inbound traffic, warehousing and stores, incoming quality control—report to a single responsible individual."

In the 291 organizations providing data for this part of the study, 70% employ the materials management (MM) concept. Table 14 presents these data, by organization size. In all size groups, at least 66% (close to two-thirds) of the organizations used a materials management organization. The percent using MM was somewhat greater in the two largest size categories (80% and 78%).

Table 15 presents the use of materials management by industry groups. In three industries all the organizations use MM: Apparel; Furniture and Fixtures; and Aerospace. In two more, it is used in at least 90%: Machinery, except Electrical (93%) and Transportation Equipment (92%). At the lower end, there were only three industries in which less than half used MM: Miscellaneous Manufacturing (43%) and Printing and Publishing, and Stone, Clay, Glass, (20% each). Thus, the materials management type organization certainly is the preferred type of organization structure.

THE FUNCTIONS INCLUDED IN MATERIALS MANAGEMENT

Inventory, Purchasing, and Warehousing and Stores are the most-common functions included in materials management, with 90%, 86%, and 84%, respectively, including them (Table 16). The function least included is Incoming Quality Control (25%); however, 45% of the organizations in the largest size category include it when they use MM. However, those very large organizations are less likely to include Inbound Traffic (50%), probably because their traffic needs are so large that they have a separate, stand-alone group handling all their transport needs. Also, only 45% of the largest organizations included Production Scheduling and Control under materials management.

Table 17 shows the functions under MM, by industry groups. Purchasing is included by at least three-fourths of the organizations in all but four of the industry groups: Textile Mill Product (20%), Apparel and Government-nonprofit (both 67%), and Fabricated Metal Products (71%). Incoming Quality Control is part of MM in all the organizations in Lumber and Wood; in 67% of the Apparel firms, and 62% of the Petroleum and Coal firms which use MM. It is part of MM in only 6% of the 18 Aerospace firms which use MM, probably due to government requirements that the purchasing and quality functions be separated.

THE CHIEF PURCHASING OFFICER (CPO)

Title
The titles carried by the Chief Purchasing Officer (CPO) vary greatly from organization to organization, and a given title is not used with consistent meaning in various organizations. The duties of a person with the title of Manager of Purchasing may be similar to another person titled Vice President of Purchasing and perhaps may encompass even greater authority and responsibility. However, title does convey some degree of status.

The most-used title is Director of Purchasing (38% have this title), followed by Vice President of Purchasing (23%), and

Manager of Purchasing (18%), (Table 18). Only two of the 297 respondents carry the title of Purchasing Agent, showing that this title almost has disappeared from the scene. A comparison with the 1960 AMA study shows the changes which have occurred.

Title	1960 AMA Study[9]	1987 CAPS Study
Purchasing Agent	47%	1%
Director of Purchases (Purchasing)	20	
General Purchasing Agent	4	
Director of Purchasing	3	38
Vice President and Director of Purchases	2	
Director of Purchasing and Stores	1	
Manager of Purchases	1	
Manager of Purchasing		18
Vice President	1	
Vice President - Purchasing	1	
Vice President of Purchasing		23
Other	17	5
Materials Manager		2
Director of Material		5
Vice President of Materials Management		9

The Vice President of Purchasing title is used by 33% of the organizations in the largest size group and 35% in the next-to-the-largest size group. It is less common in the smaller organizations. The title of Manager of Purchasing has greatest use in the small organizations, and Director of Purchasing tends to be used more commonly in the three smaller size categories.

Table 19 shows the title of the CPO, by the 23 industry groups. Only in the Lumber and Wood, and Service industries was the title of Purchasing Agent used. The title of Director of Purchasing appears throughout all industry groups and is used by over a third of all organizations in Food and Beverage (47%), Tobacco Products (80%), Textile Mill Product (50%), Furniture and Fixtures (100%), Paper (57%), Printing and Publishing (57%), Chemicals (50%), Primary Metals (53%), Machinery, except Electrical (50%), Miscellaneous Manufacturing (43%), Retail/Trade/Distribution (50%), and Service (34%).

Age

The CPO has an average age of just under 50. The average age for the total of 289 people who supplied these data was 49.3 years. The lowest average age was 46.6 years in the smallest size category and highest at 51.8 years in the next-to-the-largest size category. None of the respondents were under 30, but 16% were from 30 to 40 years old; only 7% were over age 60 (Table 20). Thirty-eight percent of the total were in the 41 to 50 age group, with an almost equal 39% in the 51 to 60 age group.

Table 21 presents the age data by industry groups. The highest average ages were in:

Industry	Average Age
Government-nonprofit	53
Tobacco Products	52
Rubber and Plastics	52
Primary Metals	52
Chemicals	51
Food and Beverage	50
Paper	50
Electric, Electronic Equipment	50
Aerospace	50

The lowest average ages were in Retail/Trade/Distribution (41), and Furniture and Fixtures (43). Thus the average ages of CPO's tend to cluster about a fairly narrow range, from 41 years to 53 years of age.

Education

The CPO's in the 295 organizations which supplied data were well educated: 94% were college graduates and 39% held an advanced degree in addition to the bachelor's degree. Table 22 presents the education of the CPO by size categories. The three largest size categories had the highest percentages of the CPO's holding advanced degrees, with 48% in the $1.1-5 billion category, 45% in the $5.1-10 billion category, and 56% in the over $10 billion category.

Table 23 presents the education of the CPO, by industry groups. The industry groups with the highest percent of CPO's holding a bachelor's degree are, in descending order:

Industry Group	Bachelor's degree only	Bachelor's and graduate degree	Total
Stone, Clay, Glass	20%	80%	100%
Lumber and Wood	33	67	100
Tobacco Products	40	60	100
Government-nonprofit	50	50	100
Retail/Trade/Distribution	50	50	100
Fabricated Metal Products	56	44	100
Machinery, except Electrical	79	21	100
Instruments and Related Products	80	20	100
Textile Mill Product	83	17	100
Apparel	100	0	100
Chemicals	47	50	97
Food and Beverage	52	45	97
Petroleum and Coal	55	41	96
Electric, Electronic Equipment	68	28	96
Service	45	48	93
Transportation Equipment	50	42	92
Rubber and Plastics	50	40	90
Aerospace	44	44	88
Primary Metals	43	43	86
Paper	43	43	86
Printing and Publishing	57	29	86
Miscellaneous Manufacturing	71	14	85
Furniture and Fixtures	33	0	33

This shows that in six of the industry groups 50% or more of the CPO's held an advanced degree, in addition to the bachelor's: Stone, Clay, Glass (80%), Lumber and Wood (67%), Tobacco Products (60%), Government-nonprofit (50%), Retail/Trade/Distribution (50%), and Chemicals (50%).

Specialization In The Bachelor's Degree

Table 24 presents the data on the subject area in which the CPO did his or her bachelor's degree work. The majority (55%) had done their work in business, followed by 19% in engineering. When compared on a size-category basis, the business area was somewhat more common in the two smaller size categories; engineering was the area of specialization by a substantially-larger percent of the CPO's in the largest two size categories than in the smaller size categories. The percentage who had specialized in liberal arts was about twice as great in the three smaller

size categories than in the two largest size categories.

Table 25 presents these data by industry groups. The percent who had specialized in business was larger than the percent in engineering in all but four industry groups: Textile Mill Product; Furniture and Fixtures; Chemicals; Stone, Clay, Glass. In the total manufacturing sector, 53% had majored in business; only 20% in engineering. But in the Service sector, the percents were 68% in business, compared to only 8% in engineering.

Years In Present Position

Table 26 presents the data on years that the CPO has been in his or her present position, by organization size. The average for the 296 respondents who supplied data was 6 years. The average for the $500 million to 1 billion category was 8, but it was only 3 years in the largest size category. In that category, 4% had been in the job for less than a year, and 81% from 1 to 5 years.

Table 27 presents the data by industry group. Only 2% had been in the job less than 1 year; 57% for 1-5 years; 23% for 6-10 years; 11% for 11-15 years; and 7% had been in the CPO position for over 15 years. The highest average years was 15 in Apparel; followed by an average of 9 in Furniture and Fixtures, Fabricated Metal Products, and Government-nonprofit; 8 in Tobacco Products, Printing and Publishing, and Rubber and Plastics; and 7 in Electric, Electronic Equipment; and Service. The lowest average years in the CPO position was in Lumber and Wood (1 year), Stone, Clay, Glass (2 years), and Aerospace and Retail/Trade/Distribution, each with 3 years.

Years With Present Employer

Table 26 shows years with present employer, by organization size. For the 297 respondents, they had an average of 18 years with their present employer, which was 3 times the 6 years they had been in their present position. The highest average years was in the largest size category, where the CPO had been with his or her firm for 23 years. The average declines steadily in the smaller size categories, going from 23, 21, 19, 17, and 15 in the smallest size category. Evidently, the CPO is a relatively-long-service employee. The averages say that he or she was with his or her employer for 12 years before assuming the CPO position. In the largest size category, he or she has been with the organization for 20 years before becoming the CPO.

Table 28 shows years with present employer, by industry group. The highest average years were in:

Furniture and Fixtures	27
Rubber and Plastics	27
Primary Metals	24
Chemicals	23
Tobacco Products	22
Apparel	21
Petroleum and Coal	21
Stone, Clay, Glass	20
Transportation Equipment	20

The lowest average years with present employer were in Lumber and Wood (9 years), Retail/Trade/Distribution (12 years), Instruments, Related Products (13 years), Machinery, except Electrical (13 years), and Service (14 years).

Years' Experience In All Functional Areas

Table 29 presents the average number of years in all functional areas, with all present and past employers, by size categories. The average years' experience, for all 295 CPO's supplying data, were, in descending order:

Purchasing	17.0	years
Operations/production	4.0	"
Marketing	1.6	"
Engineering	1.3	"
Traffic	1.0	"
Finance	0.8	"
Other	0.7	"
Accounting	0.6	"
MIS	0.5	"

The lowest number of years' experience in purchasing (12 years) was in the largest size group. These CPO's also had the lowest number of years in their present position (Table 26). The CPO's in the two largest size categories had more experience in both Operations/Production and Marketing than their counterparts in the three smaller size categories.

Table 30 presents the CPO's experience in all functional areas, by industry group. This table shows that in almost all industry groups, the CPO is very heavy in purchasing experience, with operations/production and marketing experience next in order but with relatively-few years in these areas. The 23 industry groups are listed in descending order of average years' purchasing experience, with operations/production, marketing, and engineering experience also shown.

Average years' experience in:

Industry Group	Purchasing	Opns/ Prod.	Mkt.	Eng.
Government-nonprofit	27.0	0.0	0.0	0.0
Primary Metals	22.0	1.0	1.0	0.0
Tobacco Products	21.0	4.0	0.8	0.0
Instruments, Related Products	21.0	2.0	0.0	0.0
Miscellaneous Manufacturing	20.0	2.0	0.6	1.4
Apparel	19.0	4.0	0.0	0.0
Paper	19.0	2.5	0.9	0.7
Printing and Publishing	19.0	1.0	2.7	0.7
Fabricated Metal Products	19.0	1.0	3.0	5.0
Transportation Equipment	19.0	2.0	0.5	0.6
Aerospace	19.0	5.0	0.8	0.8
Food and Beverage	18.0	3.0	0.5	1.0
Furniture and Fixtures	17.0	13.0	0.0	3.0
Machinery, except Electrical	17.0	3.0	1.6	0.5
Electric, Electronic Equipment	16.0	5.0	2.0	1.0
Chemicals	15.0	5.0	3.0	1.6
Service	15.0	4.6	1.0	1.8
Petroleum and Coal	14.0	4.0	3.0	1.8
Rubber and Plastics	13.0	5.0	1.0	2.0
Retail/Trade/Distribution	7.0	10.0	0.0	0.0
Textile Mill Product	5.0	7.0	0.0	0.2
Stone, Clay, Glass	2.6	4.0	0.8	4.0
Lumber and Wood	0.7	8.0	9.0	2.0

ORGANIZATIONAL RELATIONSHIP DATA BY INDUSTRY

To simplify the task of examining the data on purchasing organizational relationships in a specific industry, the data from the preceding tables by industry group have been rearranged to present all the information on each of the 23 specific industries in tabular form (pages 48-55). Thus the column on Food and Beverage presents the data for that specific industry in the nine data categories on which data were collected in this survey. It is hoped that this arrangement of data will be useful to those who wish to focus their attention on one specific industry.

20

FOOTNOTES

[1]"The Purchasing Agent Gains More Clout," *Business Week,* January 13, 1975, pp. 62-63.

[2]*The Kiplinger Washington Letter*, August 30, 1985, p. 3.

[3]Paul V. Farrell, C.P.M., Coordinating Editor, *Aljian's Purchasing Handbook* (New York: McGraw Hill Book Company), Fourth edition, 1982, pp. 2-8 and 2-9; George W. Aljian, *Purchasing Handbook* (New York: McGraw-Hill Book Company), Third edition, 1973, pp. 2-5 and 2-6; and George W. Aljian, Editor-in-Chief, *Purchasing Handbook* (New York: McGraw-Hill Book Company) Second edition, 1966, p. 2-10.

[4]George H. Haas, Benjamin March, and E.M. Krech, *Purchasing Department Organization and Authority*, AMA Research Study 45 (New York: American Management Association), 1960, 119 pages.

[5]*Ibid.*, p. 16-17.

[6]*Ibid.*, p. 56.

[7]George W. Aljian, *Purchasing Handbook*, Second edition, *op. cit.*

[8]*Purchasing* (December 9, 1971), p. 59.

[9]George H. Haas, Benjamin March, and E.M. Krech, *op. cit.*, p. 55.

TABLE 1
RESPONDING ORGANIZATIONS, BY INDUSTRY GROUP AND SIZE
(1986 SALES REVENUE)

						SIZE					
					Number of organizations and percent of total						
					(percent may not add to 100, due to rounding)						

INDUSTRY GROUP	Less than $500 Million		$.5-1 Billion		$1.1-5 Billion		$5.1-10 Billion		Over $10 Billion		TOTAL
	#	%	#	%	#	%	#	%	#	%	#
20 Food and beverage	6	19	7	22	12	38	4	13	3	9	32
21 Tobacco products	—		—		2	40	3	60	—		5
22 Textile mill product	3	50	—		3	50	—		—		6
23 Apparel	2	67	1	33	—		—		—		3
24 Lumber and wood	1	33	1	33	1	33	—		—		3
25 Furniture and fixtures	2	67	—		1	33	—		—		3
26 Paper	2	29	1	14	3	43	1	14	—		7
27 Printing and publishing	3	43	2	29	2	29	—		—		7
28 Chemicals	6	19	5	16	15	47	4	13	2	6	32
29 Petroleum and coal	1	5	1	5	7	32	3	14	10	45	22
30 Rubber and plastics	4	40	1	10	4	40	1	10	—		10
32 Stone, clay, glass	1	20	—		4	80	—		—		5
33 Primary metals	3	20	2	13	9	60	1	7	—		15
34 Fabricated metal products	4	44	2	22	2	22	—		1	11	9
35 Machinery, except electrical	9	64	3	21	2	14	—		—		14
36 Electric, electronic equipment	10	25	8	20	13	33	6	15	3	8	40
37 Transportation equipment	3	25	2	17	5	42	1	8	1	8	12
38 Instruments, related products	3	60	1	20	1	20	—		—		5
39 Miscellaneous manufacturing	10	71	1	7	2	14	—		1	7	14
40 Aerospace	3	17	3	17	5	28	4	22	3	17	18
TOTAL MANUFACTURING	76	29	41	16	93	35	28	11	24	9	262
5 Retail/trade/distribution	—		—		1	50	—		1	50	2
6 Government nonprofit	3	75	1	25	—		—		—		4
1 Service	5	17	3	10	16	55	3	10	2	7	29
TOTAL	84	28	45	15	110	37	31	10	27	9	297

22

TABLE 2
NUMBER OF PROFESSIONAL PURCHASING PERSONNEL, BY ORGANIZATION SIZE (1986 Sales Dollars)

NUMBER OF ORGANIZATIONS AND PERCENT
OF ORGANIZATIONS IN CATEGORY
(Percent may not add to 100, due to rounding)

NUMBER OF PROFESSIONAL PURCHASING PERSONNEL	No. Org. responding	Under $500 million		$500 mil. to $1 billion		$1.1-5 billion		$1.5-10 billion		Over $10 billion	
		#	%	#	%	#	%	#	%	#	%
25 or less	146	79	96	27	61	39	36	1	3	—	0
26-100	76	2	2	13	30	45	42	8	26	8	32
101-250	36	—	0	4	9	19	18	9	29	4	16
251-500	17	1	1	—	0	5	5	5	16	6	24
501-1,000	10	—	0	—	0	—	0	6	19	4	16
1,001 and over	5	—	0	—	0	—	0	2	6	3	12
TOTAL	290	82	99	44	100	108	101	31	99	25	100
Average number of Professional Purchasing Personnel	118	14		42		71		366		485	

TABLE 3
NUMBER OF PROFESSIONAL PURCHASING PERSONNEL, BY INDUSTRY GROUP

NUMBER OF ORGANIZATIONS IN EACH INDUSTRY GROUP,
PERCENT OF ORGANIZATIONS IN CATEGORY,
AND OVERALL AVERAGE NUMBER OF PURCHASING PROFESSIONALS
(percent may not add to 100, due to rounding)

INDUSTRY GROUP (Number of organizations responding in parentheses)		25 or less		26-100		101-250		251-500		501-1000		1001 Over		AVER-AGE
		#	%	#	%	#	%	#	%	#	%	#	%	
20 Food and beverage	(31)	22	71	4	13	5	16	—	—	—	—	—	—	42
21 Tobacco products	(5)	2	40	3	60	—	—	—	—	—	—	—	—	32
22 Textile mill product	(6)	5	83	—	—	1	17	—	—	—	—	—	—	28
23 Apparel	(3)	3	100	—	—	—	—	—	—	—	—	—	—	13
24 Lumber and wood	(2)	2	100	—	—	—	—	—	—	—	—	—	—	14
25 Furniture and fixtures	(2)	1	50	1	50	—	—	—	—	—	—	—	—	29
26 Paper	(7)	4	57	2	29	1	14	—	—	—	—	—	—	47
27 Printing and publishing	(7)	6	86	1	14	—	—	—	—	—	—	—	—	18
28 Chemicals	(31)	12	39	11	35	4	13	3	10	1	3	—	—	124
29 Petroleum and coal	(22)	8	36	9	41	2	9	2	9	1	5	—	—	97
30 Rubber and plastics	(10)	7	70	2	20	1	10	—	—	—	—	—	—	41
32 Stone, clay, glass	(5)	1	20	2	40	2	40	—	—	—	—	—	—	70
33 Primary metals	(15)	6	40	9	60	—	—	—	—	—	—	—	—	40
34 Fabricated metal products	(9)	4	44	1	11	3	33	—	—	1	11	—	—	138
35 Machinery, except electrical	(14)	12	86	—	—	1	7	1	7	—	—	—	—	43
36 Electric, electronic equip.	(39)	13	33	9	23	9	23	4	10	2	5	2	5	233
37 Transportation equipment	(12)	3	25	4	33	1	8	2	17	1	8	1	8	269
38 Instruments, related products	(5)	3	60	1	20	1	20	—	—	—	—	—	—	34
39 Miscellaneous manufacturing	(13)	10	77	2	15	—	—	1	8	—	—	—	—	54
40 Aerospace	(18)	2	11	4	22	4	22	3	17	3	17	2	11	421
TOTAL MANUFACTURING	(256)	126	49	65	25	35	14	16	6	9	4	5	2	126
5 Retail/trade/distribution	(1)	1	100	—	—	—	—	—	—	—	—	—	—	12
6 Government (nonprofit)	(4)	2	50	2	50	—	—	—	—	—	—	—	—	36
1 Service	(29)	17	59	9	31	1	3	1	3	1	3	—	—	64
TOTAL	(290)	146	50	76	26	36	12	17	6	10	3	5	2	118

TABLE 4
CENTRALIZATION AND DECENTRALIZATION OF THE
PURCHASING FUNCTION, BY ORGANIZATION SIZE
(1986 Sales Dollars)

(Percent may not add to 100, due to rounding)

ORGANIZATION STRUCTURE	No. Org. Responding		Under $500 million		$500 mil. to $1 billion		$1.1-5 billion		$5.1-10 billion		Over $10 billion	
	#	%	#	%	#	%	#	%	#	%	#	%
CENTRALIZED, in which all, or almost all, purchasing is done at one central location for the entire firm	83	28	37	44	15	33	22	20	5	16	4	15
CENTRALIZED/DECENTRALIZED, in which some purchasing is done at the corporate headquarters and purchasing also is done centrally at major operating divisions/plants	175	59	35	42	24	53	73	67	23	74	20	74
DECENTRALIZED, in which purchasing is done on a division/plant basis	38	13	12	14	6	13	14	13	3	10	3	11
TOTALS	296	100	84	100	45	99	109	100	31	100	27	100

TABLE 5
CENTRALIZATION AND DECENTRALIZATION OF THE PURCHASING FUNCTION, BY INDUSTRY GROUPS

	Centralized		Centralized/ Decentralized		Decentralized		Total
	#	%	#	%	#	%	
20 Food and beverage	15	47	17	53	0	—	32
21 Tobacco products	3	60	2	40	0	—	5
22 Textile mill product	4	67	2	33	0	—	6
23 Apparel	3	100	0	—	0	—	3
24 Lumber and wood	0	—	3	100	0	—	3
25 Furniture and fixtures	0	—	3	100	0	—	3
26 Paper	3	43	3	43	1	14	7
27 Printing and publishing	2	29	5	71	0	—	7
28 Chemicals	5	16	26	81	1	3	32
29 Petroleum and coal	4	18	17	77	1	5	22
30 Rubber and plastics	4	40	5	50	1	10	10
32 Stone, clay, glass	0	—	4	80	1	20	5
33 Primary metals	3	20	11	73	1	7	15
34 Fabricated metal products	2	22	2	22	5	56	9
35 Machinery, except electrical	3	21	6	43	5	36	14
36 Electric, electronic equipment	8	20	25	63	7	18	40
37 Transportation equipment	2	17	7	58	3	25	12
38 Instruments, related products	3	60	1	20	1	20	5
39 Miscellaneous manufacturing	2	14	6	43	6	43	14
40 Aerospace	3	17	11	61	4	22	18
TOTAL MANUFACTURING	69	26	156	60	37	14	262
5 Retail/trade/distribution	1	50	1	50	0	—	2
6 Government (nonprofit)	3	75	1	25	0	—	4
1 Service	10	36	17	61	1	4	28
TOTAL	83	28	175	59	38	13	296

FIRMS IN WHICH PURCHASING IS:
(percent may not add to 100, due to rounding)

TABLE 6
TO WHOM PURCHASING REPORTS,
BY ORGANIZATION SIZE

ORGANIZATION SIZE, 1986 SALES DOLLARS
NUMBER OF ORGANIZATIONS AND PERCENT
OF ORGANIZATIONS IN CATEGORY
(Percent may not add to 100 due to rounding)

To Whom Purchasing Reports	No. Org. Responding		Under $500 million		$500 mil. to $1 billion		$1.1-5 billion		$5.1-10 billion		Over $10 billion	
	#	%	#	%	#	%	#	%	#	%	#	%
President	47	16	11	13	7	16	18	17	10	32	1	4
Executive VP	54	18	10	12	10	22	17	16	9	29	8	31
Financial VP	21	7	7	9	1	2	7	6	1	3	5	19
Mfg/prod/opns VP	71	24	27	33	16	36	22	20	3	10	3	12
Materials Mgt VP	22	8	9	11	3	7	8	7	1	3	1	4
Engineering VP	3	1	0	—	0	—	2	2	0	—	1	4
Administrative VP	38	13	4	5	4	9	24	22	4	13	2	8
Other*	35	12	13	16	4	9	10	9	3	10	5	19
	291	99	81	99	45	101	108	99	31	100	26	101

*The 35 shown as reporting to "other" includes Division VP (6); Director of Materials (3); Materials Manager (3); Vice Chairman (3); Board of Directors (2); VP, Logistics (2); Director of Support Services (2); and 1 each to Director of Administration; Manager of Administration; Director of Manufacturing; Director of Operations; VP, Trading; VP, Systems; VP, Human Resources; VP, Engineering & Materials; Division Controller; VP, Law & Public Affairs; VP, Technical; VP, Marketing; Assistant VP; and Manager, Planning & Distribution.

TABLE 7
TO WHOM PURCHASING REPORTS, BY INDUSTRY GROUP

TITLE OF PERSON TO WHOM CHIEF PURCHASING OFFICER REPORTS
NUMBER OF ORGANIZATIONS AND PERCENT
(Percent may not add to 100, due to rounding)

	No. Organizations Responding	President		Executive VP		Financial VP		Mfg/Opns/ Prod VP		Materials Mgt. VP		Engineering VP		Administrative VP		Other	
		#	%	#	%	#	%	#	%	#	%	#	%	#	%	#	%
20 Food and beverage	31	10	32	6	19	2	6	6	19	2	6	0	—	2	6	3	10
21 Tobacco products	5	0	—	1	20	0	—	2	40	1	20	0	—	0	—	1	20
22 Textile mill product	5	0	—	2	40	0	—	1	20	0	—	1	20	1	20	0	—
23 Apparel	3	0	—	1	33	0	—	1	33	1	33	0	—	0	—	0	—
24 Lumber and wood	3	1	33	0	—	0	—	1	33	0	—	0	—	0	—	1	33
25 Furniture and fixtures	3	0	—	0	—	0	—	2	67	1	33	0	—	0	—	0	—
26 Paper	7	0	—	2	29	0	—	3	43	0	—	0	—	2	29	0	—
27 Printing and publishing	7	0	—	2	29	1	14	2	29	0	—	0	—	2	29	0	—
28 Chemicals	32	4	13	6	19	3	9	7	22	3	9	0	—	6	19	3	9
29 Petroleum and coal	22	2	9	4	18	4	18	3	14	1	5	1	5	6	27	1	5
30 Rubber and plastics	10	3	30	3	30	0	—	2	20	0	—	0	—	0	—	2	20
32 Stone, clay, glass	5	0	—	2	40	1	20	0	—	0	—	0	—	0	—	2	40
33 Primary metals	13	4	31	2	15	0	—	1	8	2	15	0	—	3	23	1	8
34 Fabricated metal products	9	3	33	3	33	0	—	0	—	0	—	0	—	1	11	2	22
35 Machinery, except electrical	14	1	7	1	7	0	—	6	43	1	7	0	—	2	14	3	21
36 Electric, electronic equipment	39	6	15	5	13	3	8	14	36	4	10	0	—	1	3	6	15
37 Transportation equipment	12	1	8	2	17	0	—	5	42	1	8	0	—	1	8	2	17
38 Instruments, related products	5	0	—	0	—	0	—	1	20	2	40	0	—	1	20	1	20
39 Miscellaneous manufacturing	14	2	14	1	7	3	21	2	14	1	7	0	—	2	14	3	21
40 Aerospace	17	3	18	4	24	0	—	6	35	1	6	0	—	2	12	1	6
TOTAL MANUFACTURING	256	40	16	47	18	17	7	65	25	21	8	2	1	32	13	32	13
5 Retail/trade/distribution	2	0	—	1	50	0	—	0	—	0	—	0	—	0	—	1	50
6 Government (nonprofit)	4	0	—	0	—	1	25	0	—	0	—	0	—	1	25	2	50
1 Service	29	7	24	6	21	3	10	6	21	1	3	1	3	5	17	0	—
TOTAL	291	47	16	54	19	21	7	71	24	22	8	3	1	38	13	35	12

TABLE 8
FUNCTIONS THAT REPORT TO PURCHASING,
BY ORGANIZATION SIZE

	ORGANIZATION SIZE, 1986 SALES DOLLARS											
	Total Organizations		Under $500 million		$500 mil. to $1 billion		$1.1-5 billion		$5.1-10 billion		Over $10 billion	
	#	%	#	%	#	%	#	%	#	%	#	%
Inbound Traffic	29	10	14	17	2	4	8	7	2	6	3	11
Outbound Traffic	2	1	0	—	0	—	2	2	0	—	0	—
Both Inbound and Outbound Traffic	91	31	18	21	16	36	32	29	13	42	12	44
Warehousing or Stores	102	34	31	37	14	31	40	36	8	26	9	33
Inventory Control	111	37	29	35	21	47	43	39	8	26	10	37
Scrap/Surplus Disposal	169	57	54	64	24	53	62	56	13	42	16	59
Receiving	77	26	24	29	15	33	29	26	4	13	5	19
Incoming Inspection	48	16	12	14	5	11	24	22	1	3	6	22
Other*	81	27	20	24	14	31	32	29	10	32	5	19
Number Organizations Responding	297		84		45		110		31		27	

*Under "Other" are included Fleet Management (11), Personnel Travel (9), Production Scheduling and Control (6), Contract Administration (5), Minority Programs (5), Office Services (4), Printing (4), Material Planning and Forecasting (4), Property Administration (4). The following functions were indicated by 3 or fewer organizations: Expediting, Pattern Shop, Aircraft, Security, Demolition, Asset Recovery, Agriculture, Engineering Standards, Equipment Specifications, Hydrocarbon Trading, Packaging Engineering, Engineering, Project Management, International Trading, and Industrial Sales.

TABLE 9
FUNCTIONS THAT REPORT TO PURCHASING, BY INDUSTRY GROUPS

	Number Orgs. Responding	Inbound Traffic		Outbound Traffic		Both Inbound and Outbound Traffic		Warehousing or Stores		Inventory Control		Scrap/Surplus Disposal		Receiving		Incoming Inspection		Other	
		#	%	#	%	#	%	#	%	#	%	#	%	#	%	#	%	#	%
20 Food and beverage	32	5	16	0	—	5	16	10	31	12	38	15	47	6	19	4	13	10	31
21 Tobacco products	5	0	—	0	—	0	—	0	—	0	—	1	20	0	—	1	20	1	20
22 Textile mill product	6	1	17	0	—	1	17	4	67	3	50	5	83	3	50	2	33	1	17
23 Apparel	3	1	33	0	—	0	—	1	33	2	67	3	100	2	67	2	67	0	—
24 Lumber and wood	3	0	—	0	—	0	—	0	—	0	—	1	33	0	—	0	—	1	33
25 Furniture and fixtures	3	1	33	0	—	0	—	2	67	0	—	2	67	1	33	0	—	0	—
26 Paper	7	1	14	0	—	1	14	5	71	5	71	5	71	3	43	0	—	1	14
27 Printing and publishing	7	0	—	0	—	1	14	3	43	3	43	5	71	4	57	3	43	3	43
28 Chemicals	32	2	6	1	3	8	25	8	25	9	28	17	53	5	16	3	9	9	28
29 Petroleum and coal	22	2	9	0	—	9	41	10	45	13	59	18	82	6	27	9	41	5	23
30 Rubber and plastics	10	1	10	0	—	3	30	5	50	9	90	7	70	3	30	0	—	2	20
32 Stone, clay, glass	5	1	20	0	—	3	60	2	40	2	40	3	60	1	20	1	20	1	20
33 Primary metals	15	0	—	0	—	6	40	5	33	6	40	13	87	3	20	3	20	1	7
34 Fabricated metal products	9	0	—	0	—	6	67	3	33	3	33	4	44	1	11	1	11	5	56
35 Machinery, except electrical	14	1	7	0	—	6	43	4	29	4	29	9	64	2	14	0	—	8	57
36 Electric, electronic equipment	40	4	10	0	—	12	30	9	23	10	25	17	43	10	25	7	18	6	15
37 Transportation equipment	12	1	8	0	—	5	42	1	8	1	8	5	42	1	8	2	17	6	50
38 Instruments, related products	5	0	—	0	—	1	20	0	—	0	—	0	—	1	20	0	—	1	20
39 Miscellaneous manufacturing	14	3	21	0	—	2	14	4	29	4	29	13	93	4	29	1	7	2	14
40 Aerospace	18	1	6	0	—	7	39	6	33	7	39	6	33	5	28	1	6	7	39
TOTAL MANUFACTURING	262	25	10	1	—	76	29	82	31	93	35	149	57	61	23	40	15	70	27
5 Retail/trade/distribution	2	1	50	0	—	0	—	0	—	0	—	1	50	0	—	0	—	0	—
6 Government (nonprofit)	4	0	—	0	—	2	50	2	50	2	50	1	25	1	25	0	—	3	75
1 Service	29	3	10	1	3	13	45	18	62	16	55	18	62	15	52	8	28	8	28
TOTAL	297	29	10	2	1	91	31	102	34	111	37	169	57	77	26	48	16	81	27

TABLE 10
ACTIVITY AREAS NEWLY ASSIGNED (SINCE 1980) TO PURCHASING, BY ORGANIZATION SIZE

	Total		Under $500 million		$500 to $1 billion		$1.1-5 billion		$5.1-10 billion		Over $10 billion	
NO. ORG. RESPONDING	292		81		44		108		31		28	
	#	%	#	%	#	%	#	%	#	%	#	%
ACTIVITY AREA												
Strategic Planning	26	9	11	14	2	5	7	6	2	6	4	14
Product Development	8	3	5	6	1	2	2	2	0	—	0	—
Traffic/Transportation	37	13	10	12	5	11	13	12	5	16	4	14
New Product Evaluation	12	4	7	9	1	2	2	2	1	3	1	4
Capital Equipment Buys	21	7	11	14	2	5	5	5	2	6	1	4
Personnel Travel	41	14	5	6	10	23	15	14	5	16	6	21
Marketing Planning	4	1	3	4	0	—	1	1	0	—	0	—
Providing Economic Forecasts/ Indicators	18	6	6	7	2	5	10	9	0	—	0	—
Commodity Futures Trading	8	3	4	5	2	5	2	2	0	—	0	—
Cash-Flow Planning	11	4	6	7	1	2	4	4	0	—	0	—
Countertrade/Offset Planning/ Execution	36	12	10	12	3	7	13	12	7	23	3	11

TABLE 11
ACTIVITY AREAS NEWLY ASSIGNED (SINCE 1980) TO PURCHASING, BY INDUSTRY GROUPS

	No. Orgs. Responding	Strategic Planning		Product Development		Traffic/ Transportation		New Product Evaluation		Capital Equip. Buys		Personnel Travel		Marketing Planning		Providing Econ. Forecasts/Indicators		Commodity Futures Trading		Cash-Flow Planning		Countertrade/Offset Planning/Execution	
		#	%	#	%	#	%	#	%	#	%	#	%	#	%	#	%	#	%	#	%	#	%
20 Food and beverage	31	2	6	1	3	2	6	0	—	1	3	3	10	0	—	0	—	2	6	1	3	2	6
21 Tobacco products	5	1	20	0	—	0	—	0	—	0	—	1	20	0	—	0	—	0	—	0	—	0	—
22 Textile mill product	6	1	17	0	—	2	33	1	17	0	—	0	—	0	—	2	33	0	—	0	—	0	—
23 Apparel	3	1	33	0	—	0	—	1	33	0	—	0	—	0	—	0	—	0	—	0	—	0	—
24 Lumber and wood	3	0	—	0	—	0	—	0	—	0	—	0	—	0	—	0	—	0	—	0	—	0	—
25 Furniture and fixtures	3	0	—	0	—	0	—	0	—	0	—	0	—	0	—	0	—	1	33	0	—	1	33
26 Paper	7	0	—	1	14	0	—	0	—	0	—	0	—	0	—	0	—	0	—	0	—	0	—
27 Printing and publishing	6	1	17	0	—	1	17	0	—	1	17	1	17	0	—	1	17	0	—	0	—	0	—
28 Chemicals	32	0	—	0	—	3	9	1	3	4	13	4	13	0	—	2	6	1	3	0	—	4	13
29 Petroleum and coal	21	1	5	0	—	3	14	0	—	0	—	3	14	0	—	0	—	0	—	0	—	1	5
30 Rubber and plastics	10	0	—	0	—	0	—	0	—	1	10	1	10	0	—	1	10	0	—	0	—	0	—
32 Stone, clay, glass	5	0	—	0	—	3	60	0	—	1	20	0	—	0	—	0	—	0	—	0	—	2	40
33 Primary metals	14	2	14	0	—	3	21	0	—	1	7	2	14	0	—	0	—	0	—	0	—	4	29
34 Fabricated metal	9	1	11	1	11	3	33	1	11	1	11	1	11	0	—	0	—	0	—	0	—	3	33
35 Machinery, except electrical	14	4	29	1	7	3	21	4	29	3	21	2	14	1	7	3	21	0	—	1	7	1	7
36 Electric, electronic equipment	40	7	18	1	3	5	13	1	3	2	5	8	20	1	3	5	13	3	8	3	8	6	15
37 Transportation equipment	12	0	—	0	—	1	8	1	8	0	—	1	8	0	—	0	—	0	—	0	—	0	—
38 Instruments, related products	5	0	—	0	—	0	—	0	—	0	—	2	40	0	—	0	—	0	—	0	—	1	20
39 Misc. mfg.	14	2	14	1	7	0	—	0	—	3	21	1	7	0	—	1	7	0	—	0	—	1	7
40 Aerospace	18	3	17	0	—	1	6	0	—	0	—	3	17	0	—	0	—	0	—	1	6	6	33
TOTAL MANUFACTURING	258	26	10	6	2	30	12	10	4	18	7	33	13	2	1	15	6	7	3	6	2	32	12
5 Retail/trade/distribution	2	0	—	0	—	1	50	1	50	1	50	1	50	0	—	0	—	0	—	0	—	0	—
6 Government (nonprofit)	3	0	—	0	—	1	33	0	—	0	—	1	33	0	—	0	—	0	—	0	—	0	—
1 Service	29	0	—	2	7	5	17	1	3	2	7	6	21	2	7	3	10	1	3	5	17	4	14
TOTAL	292	26	9	8	3	37	13	12	4	21	7	41	14	4	1	18	6	8	3	11	4	36	12

TABLE 12
ACTIVITY AREAS IN WHICH PURCHASING HAS ASSUMED AN INCREASED ROLE/RESPONSIBILITY (SINCE 1980) BY ORGANIZATION SIZE

NO. ORG. RESPONDING	Total 292		Under $500 million 81		$500 to $1 billion 44		$1.1-5 billion 108		$5.1-10 billion 31		Over $10 billion 28	
ACTIVITY AREA	#	%	#	%	#	%	#	%	#	%	#	%
Strategic Planning	125	43	29	36	27	61	49	45	11	35	9	32
Product Development	90	31	31	38	17	39	30	28	9	29	3	11
Traffic/Transportation	66	23	22	27	13	30	27	25	3	10	1	4
New Product Evaluation	77	26	24	30	15	34	31	29	5	16	2	7
Capital Equipment Buys	108	37	24	30	21	48	44	41	10	32	9	32
Personnel Travel	46	16	11	14	8	18	18	17	4	13	5	18
Marketing Planning	27	9	10	12	4	9	10	9	1	3	2	7
Providing Economic Forecasts/Indicators	120	41	34	42	19	43	50	46	7	23	10	36
Commodity Futures Trading	18	6	2	2	5	11	6	56	2	6	3	11
Cash-Flow Planning	38	13	14	17	9	20	13	12	2	6	0	—
Countertrade/Offset Planning/Execution	44	15	3	4	7	16	23	21	6	19	5	18

TABLE 13
ACTIVITY AREA IN WHICH PURCHASING HAS ASSUMED
(SINCE 1980) AN INCREASED ROLE OR RESPONSIBILITY, BY INDUSTRY GROUPS

	No. Orgs. Responding	Strategic Planning		Product Development		Traffic/ Transportation		New Product Evaluation		Capital Equipment Buys		Personnel Travel		Marketing Planning		Providing Economic Forecasts/Indicators		Commodity futures Trading		Cash-flow Planning		Countertrade/offset Planning Execution	
		#	%	#	%	#	%	#	%	#	%	#	%	#	%	#	%	#	%	#	%	#	%
20 Food and beverage	31	12	39	14	45	4	13	10	32	9	29	4	13	4	13	15	48	5	16	3	10	2	6
21 Tobacco products	5	1	20	2	40	0	—	2	40	2	40	0	—	0	—	3	60	1	20	0	—	0	—
22 Textile mill product	6	1	17	1	17	1	17	1	17	3	50	0	—	0	—	1	17	0	—	0	—	0	—
23 Apparel	3	2	67	2	67	0	—	2	67	1	33	0	—	0	—	1	33	0	—	0	—	0	—
24 Lumber and wood	3	1	33	1	33	2	67	0	—	2	67	2	67	0	—	2	67	0	—	0	—	0	—
25 Furniture and fixtures	3	1	33	2	67	1	33	2	67	2	67	0	—	0	—	1	33	0	—	0	—	0	—
26 Paper	7	5	71	3	43	4	57	1	14	4	57	0	—	2	29	6	86	0	—	2	29	2	29
27 Printing and publishing	6	3	50	2	33	0	—	2	33	3	50	3	50	1	17	4	67	0	—	0	—	0	—
28 Chemicals	32	17	53	13	41	11	34	9	28	17	53	6	19	7	22	16	50	3	9	5	16	8	25
29 Petroleum and coal	21	6	29	4	19	5	24	4	19	5	24	4	19	4	19	10	48	0	—	1	5	3	14
30 Rubber and plastics	10	4	40	1	10	1	10	2	20	1	10	0	—	1	10	5	50	2	20	2	20	2	20
32 Stone, clay, glass	5	0	—	1	20	0	—	2	40	0	—	0	—	0	—	2	40	0	—	1	20	0	—
33 Primary metals	14	5	36	2	14	4	29	5	36	5	36	2	14	1	7	7	50	1	7	3	21	4	29
34 Fabricated metal products	9	5	56	2	22	2	22	3	33	2	22	1	11	1	11	4	44	0	—	1	11	2	22
35 Machinery, except electrical	14	4	29	3	21	3	21	1	7	2	14	2	14	2	14	3	21	0	—	1	7	0	—
36 Electric, electronic equipment	40	19	48	11	28	7	18	7	18	17	43	7	18	1	3	15	38	3	8	2	5	9	23
37 Transportation equipment	12	8	67	6	50	2	17	6	50	4	33	1	8	0	—	6	50	0	—	1	8	5	42
38 Instruments, related products	5	0	—	1	20	3	60	1	20	1	20	1	20	0	—	0	—	0	—	1	20	0	—
39 Miscellaneous manufacturing	14	9	64	8	57	3	21	4	29	5	36	3	21	1	7	7	50	0	—	4	29	2	14
40 Aerospace	18	9	50	5	36	1	6	1	6	7	39	2	11	1	6	2	11	1	6	4	22	5	27
TOTAL MANUFACTURING	258	112	43	84	33	54	21	65	25	92	36	38	15	26	10	110	43	16	6	31	12	44	17
5 Retail/trade/ distribution	2	0	—	1	50	1	50	0	—	1	50	0	—	0	—	0	—	0	—	0	—	0	—
6 Government (nonprofit)	3	2	67	0	—	1	33	0	—	2	67	2	67	0	—	1	33	0	—	1	33	0	—
1 Service	29	11	38	5	17	10	34	12	41	13	45	6	21	1	3	9	31	2	7	6	21	0	—
TOTAL	292	125	43	90	31	66	23	77	26	108	37	46	16	27	9	120	41	18	6	38	13	44	15

TABLE 14
USE OF THE MATERIALS MANAGEMENT ORGANIZATION
CONCEPT, BY ORGANIZATION SIZE (1986 SALES DOLLARS)

(Percent may not add to 100, due to rounding)

	Total		Under $500 million		$500 mil. to $1 billion		$1.1-5 billion		$5.1-10 billion		Over $10 billion	
			#	%	#	%	#	%	#	%	#	%
Organization DOES USE Materials Management Concept	204	70	58	70	29	66	71	67	24	80	22	78
Organization DOES NOT USE Materials Management Concept	87	30	25	30	15	34	35	33	6	20	6	22
TOTALS	291	100	83	100	44	100	106	100	30	100	28	100

TABLE 15
USE OF THE MATERIALS MANAGEMENT CONCEPT, BY INDUSTRY GROUP

	Number of Organizations Responding	Number and Percent *Using* Materials Management		Number and Percent *Not Using* Materials Management	
		#	%	#	%
20 Food and beverage	31	16	52	15	48
21 Tobacco products	5	4	80	1	20
22 Textile mill product	6	5	83	1	17
23 Apparel	3	3	100	0	0
24 Lumber and wood	3	2	67	1	33
25 Furniture and fixtures	3	3	100	0	0
26 Paper	7	5	71	2	29
27 Printing and publishing	5	1	20	4	80
28 Chemicals	32	23	72	9	28
29 Petroleum and coal	22	13	59	9	41
30 Rubber and plastics	10	8	80	2	20
32 Stone, clay, glass	5	1	20	4	80
33 Primary metals	14	9	64	5	36
34 Fabricated metal products	9	7	78	2	22
35 Machinery, except electrical	14	13	93	1	7
36 Electric, electronic equipment	40	29	73	11	28
37 Transportation equipment	12	11	92	1	8
38 Instruments, related products	5	3	60	2	40
39 Miscellaneous manufacturing	14	6	43	8	57
40 Aerospace	18	18	100	0	0
TOTAL MANUFACTURING	258	180	70	78	30
5 Retail/trade/distribution	1	0	0	1	100
6 Government (nonprofit)	4	3	75	1	25
1 Service	28	21	75	7	25
TOTAL	291	204	70	87	30

TABLE 16
FUNCTIONS INCLUDED UNDER THE MATERIALS MANAGER, BY ORGANIZATION SIZE (1986 SALES DOLLARS)

FUNCTION	Total		Under $500 million		$500 to $1 billion		$1.1-5 billion		$5.1-10 billion		Over $10 billion	
	#	%	#	%	#	%	#	%	#	%	#	%
Number organizations using MM	204		58		29		71		24		22	
Purchasing	175	86	44	76	29	100	61	86	23	96	18	82
Inventory	184	90	52	90	28	97	63	89	22	92	19	86
Production scheduling and control	121	59	33	57	18	62	48	68	12	50	10	45
Inbound traffic	137	67	39	67	22	76	48	68	17	71	11	50
Warehousing and stores	172	84	52	90	27	93	58	82	18	75	17	77
Incoming quality control	51	25	11	19	7	24	18	25	5	21	10	45

TABLE 17
FUNCTIONS INCLUDED UNDER THE MATERIALS MANAGER, BY INDUSTRY GROUP

	No. Org. Using MM	Purchasing		Inventory		Production Scheduling & Control		Inbound Traffic		Warehousing & Stores		Incoming Quality Control	
		#	%	#	%	#	%	#	%	#	%	#	%
20 Food and beverage	16	14	88	15	94	10	63	9	56	13	81	4	25
21 Tobacco products	4	4	100	2	50	1	25	2	50	3	75	1	25
22 Textile mill product	5	1	20	4	80	1	20	1	20	4	80	0	0
23 Apparel	3	2	67	2	67	1	33	1	33	1	33	2	67
24 Lumber and wood	2	2	100	1	50	1	50	1	50	2	100	2	100
25 Furniture and fixtures	3	3	100	3	100	2	67	1	33	3	100	1	33
26 Paper	5	5	100	5	100	3	60	4	80	5	100	0	0
27 Printing and publishing	1	1	100	0	0	1	100	1	100	0	0	0	0
28 Chemicals	23	19	83	19	83	19	83	20	87	21	91	1	4
29 Petroleum and coal	13	10	77	13	100	1	8	6	46	12	92	8	62
30 Rubber and plastics	8	7	88	5	63	5	63	5	63	5	63	0	0
32 Stone, clay, glass	1	1	100	1	100	1	100	1	100	1	100	0	0
33 Primary metals	9	9	100	8	89	4	44	6	67	7	78	3	33
34 Fabricated metal products	7	5	71	7	100	7	100	3	43	7	100	2	29
35 Machinery, except electrical	13	10	77	12	92	11	85	11	85	13	100	3	23
36 Electric, electronic equipment	29	29	100	28	97	22	76	24	83	24	83	12	41
37 Transportation equipment	11	10	91	10	91	8	73	8	73	7	64	0	0
38 Instruments, related products	3	3	100	3	100	3	100	2	67	2	67	0	0
39 Miscellaneous manufacturing	6	6	100	6	100	4	67	3	50	6	100	1	17
40 Aerospace	18	14	78	16	89	9	50	12	67	12	67	1	6
TOTAL MANUFACTURING	180	155	86	160	89	114	63	121	67	149	83	41	23
5 Retail/trade/distribution	0	0	—	0	—	0	—	0	—	0	—	0	—
6 Government (nonprofit)	3	2	67	3	100	0	—	3	100	3	100	0	—
1 Service	21	18	86	21	100	7	33	13	62	20	95	10	48
TOTAL	204	175	86	184	90	121	59	137	67	172	85	51	25

TABLE 18
TITLE OF CHIEF PURCHASING OFFICER, BY COMPANY SIZE

TITLE	Under $500 million		$500 mil. to $1 billion		$1.1-5 billion		$5.1-10 billion		Over $10 billion		TOTAL	
	#	%	#	%	#	%	#	%	#	%	#	%
Purchasing Agent	2	2	—	0	—	0	—	0	—	0	2	1
Manager of Purchasing	31	37	3	7	9	8	2	6	7	26	52	18
Director of Purchasing	33	39	22	49	46	42	8	26	3	11	112	38
Vice President of Purchasing	5	6	8	18	34	31	11	35	9	33	67	23
Materials Manager	5	6	—	0	1	1	—	0	—	0	6	2
Director of Material	2	2	4	9	4	4	3	10	3	11	16	5
Vice President of Materials Management	4	5	6	13	7	6	6	19	3	11	26	9
Other*	2	2	2	4	9	8	1	3	2	7	16	5
TOTAL	84	99	45	100	110	100	31	99	27	99	297	101

Company Size, 1986 Sales Dollars
(Percent may not add to 100, due to rounding)

*The 16 titles under "Other" were VP, Logistics (3); Assistant VP (2); Director, Corporate Services (2); and 1 each VP, Sourcing; VP, Support Services; Director, Operations; VP, Materials Acquisition; VP, Manufacturing; VP, Supply; VP, Operations; Administrative Manager; and VP, Technical.

TABLE 19
TITLE OF CHIEF PURCHASING OFFICER, BY INDUSTRY GROUP

NUMBER OF ORGANIZATIONS IN WHICH
TITLE USED AND PERCENT
(percent may not add to 100, due to rounding)

	# of Organizations Responding	Purchasing Agent		Manager of Purchasing		Director of Purchasing		Vice President of Purchasing		Materials Manager		Director of Material		Vice President of Materials Mgmt.		Other	
		#	%	#	%	#	%	#	%	#	%	#	%	#	%	#	%
20 Food and beverage	32	—	—	3	.9	15	47	11	34	—	—	—	—	2	6	1	3
21 Tobacco products	5	—	—	—	—	4	80	1	20	—	—	—	—	—	—	—	—
22 Textile mill product	6	—	—	—	—	3	50	2	33	—	—	1	17	—	—	—	—
23 Apparel	3	—	—	—	—	1	33	2	67	—	—	—	—	—	—	—	—
24 Lumber and wood	3	1	33	—	—	1	33	—	—	—	—	—	—	—	—	1	33
25 Furniture and fixtures	3	—	—	—	—	3	100	—	—	—	—	—	—	—	—	—	—
26 Paper	7	—	—	—	—	4	57	2	29	1	14	—	—	—	—	—	—
27 Printing and publishing	7	—	—	1	14	4	57	1	14	—	—	1	14	—	—	—	—
28 Chemicals	32	—	—	2	6	16	50	10	31	—	—	—	—	2	6	2	6
29 Petroleum and coal	22	—	—	12	55	3	14	2	9	1	5	1	5	1	5	2	9
30 Rubber and plastics	10	—	—	2	20	3	30	3	30	—	—	—	—	2	20	—	—
32 Stone, clay, glass	5	—	—	—	—	1	20	4	80	—	—	—	—	—	—	—	—
33 Primary metals	15	—	—	1	7	8	53	4	27	—	—	1	7	—	—	1	7
34 Fabricated metal products	9	—	—	1	11	3	33	2	22	—	—	—	—	2	22	1	11
35 Machinery, except electrical	14	—	—	3	21	7	50	1	7	2	14	—	—	1	7	—	—
36 Electric, electronic equip.	40	—	—	8	20	12	30	7	18	1	3	7	18	4	10	1	3
37 Transportation equipment	12	—	—	4	33	4	33	2	17	—	—	—	—	1	8	1	8
38 Instruments, related products	5	—	—	2	40	1	20	—	—	—	—	—	—	—	—	2	40
39 Miscellaneous manufacturing	14	—	—	5	36	6	43	1	7	1	7	—	—	—	—	1	7
40 Aerospace	18	—	—	4	22	1	6	2	11	—	—	3	17	7	39	1	6
TOTAL MANUFACTURING	262	1	0	48	18	100	38	57	22	6	2	14	5	22	8	14	5
5 Retail/trade/distribution	2	—	—	—	—	1	50	1	50	—	—	—	—	—	—	—	—
6 Government (nonprofit)	4	—	—	3	75	1	25	—	—	—	—	—	—	—	—	—	—
1 Service	29	1	3	1	3	10	34	9	31	—	—	2	7	4	14	2	7
TOTAL	297	2	1	52	18	112	38	67	23	6	2	16	5	26	9	16	5

TABLE 20
AGE OF CHIEF PURCHASING OFFICER, BY ORGANIZATION SIZE

	Under $500 million		$500 to $1 billion		$1.1-5 billion		$5.1-10 billion		Over $10 billion		*Total	
Number of Organizations Responding	83		44		105		30		27		289	
	#	%	#	%	#	%	#	%	#	%	#	%
AGE RANGE												
30-40	24	29	4	9	12	11	2	7	4	15	46	16
41-50	30	36	19	43	38	36	14	47	8	30	109	38
51-60	27	33	16	36	47	45	10	33	14	52	114	39
Over 60	2	2	5	11	8	8	4	13	1	4	20	7
AVERAGE AGE	46.6		49.6		50.5		51.8		49.5		49.3	

*Eight organizations did not supply data.

TABLE 21
AGE OF CHIEF PURCHASING OFFICER, BY INDUSTRY GROUPS

	No. Orgs Responding	30-40 #	30-40 %	41-50 #	41-50 %	51-60 #	51-60 %	Over 60 #	Over 60 %	Average Age
		AGE OF CHIEF PURCHASING OFFICER (Percents may not add to 100, due to rounding)								
20 Food and beverage	31	3	10	13	42	14	45	1	3	50
21 Tobacco products	5	0	—	2	40	3	60	0	—	52
22 Textile mill product	6	2	33	3	50	0	—	1	17	46
23 Apparel	3	1	33	1	33	1	33	0	—	46
24 Lumber and wood	3	1	33	1	33	1	33	0	—	46
25 Furniture and fixtures	3	1	33	1	33	1	33	0	—	43
26 Paper	7	0	—	3	43	3	43	1	14	50
27 Printing and publishing	7	1	14	3	43	2	29	1	14	48
28 Chemicals	32	3	9	10	31	17	53	2	6	51
29 Petroleum and coal	22	2	9	12	55	8	36	0	—	48
30 Rubber and plastics	10	2	20	1	10	7	70	0	—	52
32 Stone, clay, glass	5	2	40	2	40	1	20	0	—	46
33 Primary metals	13	2	15	1	8	9	69	1	8	52
34 Fabricated metal products	8	1	13	4	50	1	13	2	25	49
35 Machinery, except electrical	14	3	21	6	43	5	36	0	—	47
36 Electronic, electronic equipment	40	5	13	18	45	13	33	4	10	50
37 Transportation equipment	11	3	27	3	27	3	27	2	18	49
38 Instruments, related products	4	1	25	2	50	1	25	0	—	48
39 Miscellaneous manufacturing	14	4	29	5	36	4	29	1	7	48
40 Aerospace	18	2	11	8	44	5	28	3	17	50
TOTAL MANUFACTURING	256	39	15	99	39	99	39	19	7	49
5 Retail/trade/distribution	2	1	50	1	50	0	—	0	—	41
6 Government (nonprofit)	4	0	—	1	25	3	75	0	—	53
1 Service	27	6	22	8	30	12	44	1	4	49
TOTAL	289*	46	16	109	38	114	39	20	7	49

*Eight organizations did not supply data.

TABLE 22
EDUCATION OF CHIEF PURCHASING OFFICER, BY ORGANIZATION SIZE

EDUCATION	Total #	Total %	Under $500 million #	Under $500 million %	$500 mil. to $1 billion #	$500 mil. to $1 billion %	$1.1-5 billion #	$1.1-5 billion %	$5.1-10 billion #	$5.1-10 billion %	Over $10 billion #	Over $10 billion %
	1986 Sales Dollars											
High School	19	6	5	6	7	16	3	3	2	6	2	7
Bachelor's Degree	161	55	57	69	25	56	54	50	15	48	10	37
Bachelor's and Graduate Degree	115	39	21	25	13	29	52	48	14	45	15	56
TOTAL	295		83		45		109		31		27	

Percent totals may not add to 100 due to rounding.

TABLE 23
EDUCATION OF CHIEF PURCHASING OFFICER, BY INDUSTRY GROUP

	Number of Respondents	High School		Bachelor's Degree		Bachelor's and Graduate Degree	
		#	%	#	%	#	%
20 Food and beverage	31	1	3	16	52	14	45
21 Tobacco products	5	0	—	2	40	3	60
22 Textile mill product	6	0	—	5	83	1	17
23 Apparel	3	0	—	3	100	0	—
24 Lumber and wood	3	0	—	1	33	2	67
25 Furniture and fixtures	3	2	67	1	33	0	—
26 Paper	7	1	14	3	43	3	43
27 Printing and publishing	7	1	14	4	57	2	29
28 Chemicals	32	1	3	15	47	16	50
29 Petroleum and coal	22	1	5	12	55	9	41
30 Rubber and plastics	10	1	10	5	50	4	40
32 Stone, clay, glass	5	0	—	1	20	4	80
33 Primary metals	14	2	14	6	43	6	43
34 Fabricated metal products	9	0	—	5	56	4	44
35 Machinery, except electrical	14	0	—	11	79	3	21
36 Electric, electronic equipment	40	2	5	27	68	11	28
37 Transportation equipment	12	1	8	6	50	5	42
38 Instruments, related products	5	0	—	4	80	1	20
39 Miscellaneous manufacturing	14	2	14	10	71	2	14
40 Aerospace	18	2	11	8	44	8	44
TOTAL MANUFACTURING	260	17	7	145	56	98	38
5 Retail/trade/distribution	2	0	—	1	50	1	50
6 Government (nonprofit)	4	0	—	2	50	2	50
1 Service	29	2	7	13	45	14	48
TOTAL	295	19	6	161	55	115	39

TABLE 24
SPECIALIZATION IN BACHELOR'S DEGREE WORK, BY ORGANIZATION SIZE

	1986 Sales Dollars											
Area of specialization in the Bachelor's degree	Total		Under $500 million		$500 mil. to $1 billion		$1.1-5 billion		$5.1-10 billion		Over $10 billion	
	#	%	#	%	#	%	#	%	#	%	#	%
Business	147	55	47	63	24	63	53	52	11	41	12	50
Engineering	50	19	5	7	5	13	20	20	11	41	9	38
Liberal Arts	34	13	12	16	4	11	14	14	2	7	2	8
Other	35	13	11	15	5	13	15	15	3	11	1	4
TOTAL	266*		75		38		102		27		24	

*10 of the 276 CPO's holding a bachelor's degree did not supply information.

TABLE 25
SPECIALIZATION IN BACHELOR'S DEGREE WORK,
BY INDUSTRY GROUP

| | | Number of Respondents | SPECIALIZATION ON THE BACHELOR'S DEGREE | | | | | | | |
| | | | Business | | Engineering | | Liberal Arts | | Other | |
			#	%	#	%	#	%	#	%
20	Food and beverage	30	18	60	5	17	2	7	5	17
21	Tobacco products	5	3	60	0	—	0	—	2	40
22	Textile mill product	6	2	33	2	33	2	33	0	—
23	Apparel	3	2	67	0	—	1	33	0	—
24	Lumber and wood	3	2	67	1	33	0	—	0	—
25	Furniture and fixtures	1	0	—	1	100	0	—	0	—
26	Paper	6	4	67	1	17	0	—	1	17
27	Printing and publishing	6	5	83	0	—	1	17	0	—
28	Chemicals	30	10	33	10	33	5	17	5	17
29	Petroleum and coal	21	10	48	6	29	1	5	4	19
30	Rubber and plastics	8	3	38	2	25	1	13	2	25
32	Stone, clay, glass	5	1	20	2	40	1	20	1	20
33	Primary metals	12	6	50	4	33	2	17	0	—
34	Fabricated metal products	8	5	63	1	13	1	13	1	13
35	Machinery, except electrical	14	7	50	2	14	1	7	4	29
36	Electric, electronic equipment	36	20	56	6	17	7	19	3	8
37	Transportation equipment	11	8	73	1	9	1	9	1	9
38	Instruments, related products	4	2	50	0	—	1	25	1	25
39	Miscellaneous manufacturing	11	6	55	2	18	3	27	0	—
40	Aerospace	15	11	73	2	13	1	7	1	7
	TOTAL MANUFACTURING	235	125	53	48	20	31	13	31	13
5	Retail/trade/distribution	2	2	100	0	—	0	—	0	—
6	Government (nonprofit)	4	3	75	0	—	0	—	1	25
1	Service	25	17	68	2	8	3	12	3	12
	TOTAL	266	147	55	50	19	34	13	35	13

TABLE 26
THE CHIEF PURCHASING OFFICER: YEARS IN PRESENT POSITION AND YEARS WITH PRESENT EMPLOYER, BY ORGANIZATION SIZE

YEARS IN PRESENT POSITION	Total		Under $500 million		$500 mil. to $1 billion		$1.1-5 billion		$5.1-10 billion		Over $10 billion	
	#	%	#	%	#	%	#	%	#	%	#	%
Less than 1 year	6	2	2	2	1	2	2	2	0	—	1	4
1-5 years	170	57	45	54	19	42	62	56	22	71	22	81
6-10 years	67	23	20	24	13	29	29	26	3	10	2	7
11-15 years	33	11	7	8	5	11	16	15	4	13	1	4
Over 15 years	20	7	9	11	7	16	1	1	2	6	1	4
TOTAL	296	100	83*		45		110		31		27	
Average Years	6		7		8		6		5		3	

*One respondent did not supply data.

YEARS WITH PRESENT EMPLOYER	#	%	#	%	#	%	#	%	#	%	#	%
Less than 1 year	2	1	2	2	0	—	0	—	0	—	0	—
1-5 years	35	12	12	14	7	16	9	8	6	19	1	4
6-10 years	56	19	19	23	10	22	22	20	2	6	3	11
11-15 years	40	13	16	19	4	9	18	16	2	6	0	—
Over 15 years	164	55	35	42	24	53	61	55	21	68	23	85
TOTAL	297		84		45		110		31		27	
Average Years	18		15		17		19		21		23	

TABLE 27
THE CHIEF PURCHASING OFFICER:
YEARS IN PRESENT POSITION,
BY INDUSTRY GROUP

	Number of Respondents	Average Years	Under 1 Year		1-5 Years		6-10 Years		11-15 Years		Over 15 Years	
			#	%	#	%	#	%	#	%	#	%
20 Food and beverage	32	6	2	6	15	47	7	22	6	19	2	6
21 Tobacco products	5	8	0	—	2	40	1	20	2	40	0	—
22 Textile mill product	6	4	0	—	5	83	1	17	0	—	0	—
23 Apparel	3	15	0	—	1	33	1	33	0	—	1	33
24 Lumber and wood	3	1	0	—	3	100	0	—	0	—	0	—
25 Furniture and fixtures	3	9	0	—	1	33	1	33	1	33	0	—
26 Paper	7	5	0	—	4	57	2	29	1	14	0	—
27 Printing and publishing	7	8	0	—	3	43	2	29	1	14	1	14
28 Chemicals	32	6	0	—	20	63	4	13	6	19	2	6
29 Petroleum and coal	22	5	0	—	16	73	3	14	2	9	1	5
30 Rubber and plastics	10	8	0	—	5	50	2	20	1	10	2	20
32 Stone, clay, glass	5	2	0	—	5	100	0	—	0	—	0	—
33 Primary metals	15	6	0	—	9	60	5	33	1	7	0	—
34 Fabricated metal products	9	9	0	—	4	44	1	11	2	22	2	22
35 Machinery, except electrical	14	6	0	—	8	57	5	36	0	—	1	7
36 Electric, electronic equipment	39	7	1	3	21	54	8	21	4	10	5	13
37 Transportation equipment	12	6	0	—	5	42	7	58	0	—	0	—
38 Instruments, related products	5	5	0	—	3	60	1	20	1	20	0	—
39 Miscellaneous manufacturing	14	6	0	—	8	57	5	36	0	—	1	7
40 Aerospace	18	3	1	6	14	78	2	11	1	6	0	—
TOTAL MANUFACTURING	261	6	4	2	152	58	58	22	29	11	18	7
5 Retail/trade/distribution	2	3	0	—	2	100	0	—	0	—	0	—
6 Government (nonprofit)	4	9	0	—	2	50	1	25	0	—	1	25
1 Service	29	7	2	7	14	48	8	28	4	14	1	3
TOTAL	296	6	6	2	170	57	67	23	33	11	20	7

*One respondent did not supply data.

44

TABLE 28
THE CHIEF PURCHASING OFFICER: YEARS WITH PRESENT EMPLOYER, BY INDUSTRY GROUP

		Number of Respondents	Average Years	Under 1 Year		1-5 Years		6-10 Years		11-15 Years		Over 15 Years	
				#	%	#	%	#	%	#	%	#	%
20	Food and beverage	32	17	1	3	6	19	6	19	3	9	16	50
21	Tobacco products	5	22	0	—	0	—	1	20	0	—	4	80
22	Textile mill product	6	16	0	—	1	17	1	17	2	33	2	33
23	Apparel	3	21	0	—	1	33	0	—	0	—	2	67
24	Lumber and wood	3	9	0	—	0	—	3	100	0	—	0	—
25	Furniture and fixtures	3	27	0	—	0	—	0	—	1	33	2	67
26	Paper	7	18	0	—	1	14	1	14	1	14	4	57
27	Printing and publishing	7	17	0	—	0	—	1	14	3	43	3	43
28	Chemicals	32	23	0	—	3	9	1	3	7	22	21	66
29	Petroleum and coal	22	21	0	—	1	5	4	18	1	5	16	73
30	Rubber and plastics	10	27	0	—	0	—	0	—	2	20	8	80
32	Stone, clay, glass	5	20	0	—	0	—	2	40	0	—	3	60
33	Primary metals	15	24	0	—	1	7	1	7	1	7	12	80
34	Fabricated metal products	9	17	0	—	3	33	0	—	2	22	4	44
35	Machinery, except electrical	14	13	0	—	3	21	2	14	3	21	6	43
36	Electric, electronic equipment	40	16	0	—	5	13	13	33	2	5	20	50
37	Transportation equipment	12	20	0	—	0	—	2	17	3	25	7	58
38	Instruments, related products	5	13	0	—	1	20	1	20	0	—	3	60
39	Miscellaneous manufacturing	14	15	0	—	2	14	3	21	2	14	7	50
40	Aerospace	18	17	0	—	3	17	4	22	2	11	9	50
	TOTAL MANUFACTURING	262	19	1	0	31	12	46	18	35	13	149	57
5	Retail/trade/distribution	2	12	0	—	1	50	0	—	0	—	1	50
6	Government (nonprofit)	4	16	0	—	0	—	2	50	0	—	2	50
1	Service	29	14	1	3	3	10	8	28	5	17	12	41
	TOTAL	297	18	2	1	35	12	56	19	40	13	164	55

TABLE 29
THE CHIEF PURCHASING OFFICER: YEARS' EXPERIENCE
IN ALL FUNCTIONAL AREAS, BY ORGANIZATION SIZE

FUNCTIONAL AREA	Total	Under $500 million	$500 mil. to $1 billion	$1.1-5 billion	$5.1-10 billion	Over $10 billion
Purchasing	17	17	20	17	15	12
Operations/production	4	4	2.5	3.6	6	6
Engineering	1.3	.6	.7	2	1.5	1.4
Marketing	1.6	1.4	1	1.3	2.3	2.9
Finance	.8	.3	.3	1	1.7	.9
MIS	.5	.8	.2	.6	.2	.3
Traffic	1	1.3	.8	1	.5	.7
Accounting	.6	.9	.2	.6	.4	.2
Other	.7	.1	.3	1	1.6	1
Total Responses	295	83	45	109	31	27

TABLE 30
THE CHIEF PURCHASING OFFICER: YEARS' EXPERIENCE IN ALL FUNCTIONAL AREAS, BY INDUSTRY GROUP

	Number of Respondents	Purchasing	Operations/ Production	Engineering	Marketing	Finance	MIS	Traffic	Accounting	Other
20 Food and beverage	31	18	3	1	.5	.6	.3	.2	.3	1
21 Tobacco products	5	21	4	0	.8	0	0	0	0	1
22 Textile mill product	6	5	7	.2	0	0	8	.5	0	2.5
23 Apparel	3	19	4	0	0	0	0	0	0	0
24 Lumber and wood	3	.7	8	2	9	0	0	1	0	0
25 Furniture and fixtures	3	17	13	3	0	0	0	6	0	0
26 Paper	7	19	2.5	.7	.9	3	0	.3	.1	0
27 Printing and publishing	7	19	1	.7	2.7	0	.4	1.7	0	0
28 Chemicals	32	15	5	1.6	3	.6	.4	.4	.3	.9
29 Petroleum and coal	22	14	4	1.8	3	.1	.2	.7	1	.3
30 Rubber and plastics	10	13	5	2	1	2	2	3	4	0
32 Stone, clay, glass	5	2.6	4	4	.8	6	.4	0	3	0
33 Primary metals	15	22	1	0	1	1.5	.7	2	0	0
34 Fabricated metal products	9	19	1	5	3	.3	0	.9	.2	0
35 Machinery, except electrical	14	17	3	.5	1.6	0	.3	.8	.2	2
36 Electric, electronic equipment	40	16	5	1	2	1	.6	1.4	1	1
37 Transportation equipment	12	19	2	.6	.5	1.6	.8	2.5	.6	.2
38 Instruments, related products	5	21	2	0	0	0	0	2	0	4
39 Miscellaneous manufacturing	14	20	2	1.4	.6	0	.2	0	0	1
40 Aerospace	18	19	5	.8	.8	.7	.1	2	0	0
TOTAL MANUFACTURING	261	17	4	1.3	1.6	.8	.6	1	.6	.7
5 Retail/trade/distribution	2	7	10	0	0	0	0	3.5	0	0
6 Government (nonprofit)	4	27	0	0	0	0	0	0	0	0
1 Service	28	15	4.6	1.8	1	.3	0	0	.2	.5
TOTAL	295	17	4	1.3	1.6	.8	.5	1	.6	.7

47

ORGANIZATIONAL RELATIONSHIP DATA BY INDUSTRY

INDUSTRY	Food & Beverage No. of Orgs. Responding	Percent	Tobacco Products No. of Orgs. Responding	Percent	Textile Mill Product No. of Orgs. Responding	Percent	Apparel No. of Orgs. Responding	Percent	Lumber and Wood No. of Orgs. Responding	Percent	Furniture & Fixtures No. of Orgs. Responding	Percent
1. Responding Organizations, 1986 $ Sales												
A. Less than $500 million	6	19	0	0	3	50	2	67	1	33	2	67
B. $500 million to 1 billion	7	22	0	0	0	0	1	33	1	33	0	0
C. $1.1 billion to 5 billion	12	38	2	40	3	50	0	0	1	33	1	33
D. $5.1 billion to 10 billion	4	13	3	60	0	0	0	0	0	0	0	0
E. Over $10 billion	3	9	0	0	0	0	0	0	0	0	0	0
Total Respondents	32	101%	5	100%	6	100%	3	100%	3	99%	3	100%
2. Number of Professional Purchasing Personnel												
A. 25 or less	22	71	2	40	5	83	3	100	2	100	1	50
B. 26 to 100	4	13	3	60	0	0	0	0	0	0	1	50
C. 101 to 250	5	16	0	0	1	17	0	0	0	0	0	0
D. 251 to 500	0	0	0	0	0	0	0	0	0	0	0	0
E. 501 to 1,000	0	0	0	0	0	0	0	0	0	0	0	0
F. 1,001 and over	0	0	0	0	0	0	0	0	0	0	0	0
Total Respondents	31	100%	5	100%	6	100%	3	100%	2	100%	2	100%
Average number of purchasing professionals:	42		32		28		13		14		29	
3. Organizational Structure												
A. Centralized	15	47	3	60	4	67	3	100	0	0	0	0
B. Centralized/Decentralized	17	53	2	40	2	33	0	0	3	100	3	100
C. Decentralized	0	0	0	0	0	0	0	0	0	0	0	0
Total Responding	32	100%	5	100%	6	100%	3	100%	3	100%	3	100%
4. Reporting Relationships of Purchasing Purchasing reports to:												
A. President	10	32	0	0	0	0	0	0	1	33	0	0
B. Executive VP	6	19	1	20	2	40	1	33	0	0	0	0
C. Financial VP	2	6	0	0	1	20	0	0	0	0	0	0
D. Mfg./Opers./Prod. VP	6	19	2	40	0	0	1	33	1	33	2	67
E. Materials Mgmt. VP	2	6	1	20	1	20	1	33	0	0	1	33
F. Engineering VP	0	0	0	0	0	0	0	0	0	0	0	0
G. Administrative VP	2	6	0	0	1	20	0	0	0	0	0	0
H. Other	3	10	1	20	0	0	0	0	1	33	0	0
Total Respondents	31	98%	5	100%	5	100%	3	99%	3	99%	3	100%
5. Functions Reporting to Purchasing												
A. Inbound traffic only	5	16%	0	0%	1	17%	1	33%	0	0	1	33%
B. Outbound traffic only	0	0	0	0	0	0	0	0	0	0	0	0
C. Inbound and outbound traffic	5	16	0	0	4	17	1	33	0	0	0	0
D. Warehousing and stores	10	31	0	0	3	67	1	33	2	33	2	67
E. Inventory control	12	38	0	0	5	50	2	67	1	67	2	67
F. Scrap/surplus disposal	15	47	1	20	5	83	3	100	3	100	2	67
G. Receiving	6	19	0	0	2	50	2	67	2	67	1	33
H. Incoming inspection	4	13	1	20	2	33	2	67	2	67	0	0
I. Other	10	31	1	20	1	17	0	0	1	33	1	33
Total Respondents	32		5		6		3		3		3	

6. Activity Areas Newly Assigned to Purchasing and Activity Areas in Which Purchasing Has Assumed an Increased Role/Responsibility (Since 1980).

	Food & Beverage Newly Assigned No.	%	Increased Role/Resp. No.	%	Tobacco Products Newly Assigned No.	%	Increased Role/Resp. No.	%	Textile Mill Product Newly Assigned No.	%	Increased Role/Resp. No.	%	Apparel Newly Assigned No.	%	Increased Role/Resp. No.	%	Lumber and Wood Newly Assigned No.	%	Increased Role/Resp. No.	%	Furniture & Fixtures Newly Assigned No.	%	Increased Role/Resp. No.	%
A. Strategic planning	2	6	12	39	1	20	2	17	0	0	3	17	1	33	2	67	0	0	1	33	0	0	1	33
B. Product development	1	3	14	45	0	0	2	17	0	0	2	17	0	0	2	67	0	0	2	67	0	0	2	67
C. Traffic/transportation	2	6	4	13	2	33	1	17	2	33	2	67	1	33	1	33	0	0	2	67	0	0	1	33
D. New product evaluation	1	3	10	32	0	0	1	17	0	0	2	67	0	0	2	67	0	0	2	67	0	0	2	67
E. Capital equipment buys	3	10	9	29	0	0	3	50	0	0	1	33	0	0	1	33	0	0	2	67	0	0	2	67
F. Personnel travel	0	0	4	13	0	0	0	0	0	0	0	0	0	0	0	0	0	0	0	0	0	0	0	0
G. Marketing planning	0	0	4	13	2	33	0	0	0	0	1	17	2	33	0	0	0	0	0	0	0	0	0	0
H. Providing economic forecasts/indicators	2	6	15	48	0	0	3	60	0	0	1	17	0	0	1	33	0	0	2	67	1	33	0	0
I. Commodity futures trading	2	6	5	16	0	0	1	20	0	0	1	17	0	0	0	0	0	0	0	0	1	33	0	0
J. Cash-flow planning	1	3	3	10	0	0	0	0	0	0	1	17	0	0	0	0	0	0	0	0	0	0	0	0
K. Countertrade/offset planning/executing																								

7. ...rials Management Concepts												
A. Use materials management	16	52	4	80	5	83	3	100	2	67	3	100
B. Don't use materials management	15	48	1	20	1	17	0	0	1	33	0	0
Total Respondents	31	100%	5	100%	6	100%	3	100%	3	100%	3	100%
8. Functions Included Under the Materials Manager, in the Organizations Using Materials Management:												
A. Purchasing	14	88%	4	100%	1	20%	2	67%	2	100%	2	100%
B. Inventory	15	94	2	50	4	80	2	67	1	50	3	100
C. Production scheduling and control	10	63	1	25	1	20	1	33	1	50	2	67
D. Inbound traffic	9	56	2	50	1	20	1	33	1	50	1	33
E. Warehousing and stores	13	81	3	75	4	80	1	33	2	100	2	100
F. Incoming quality control	4	25	1	25	0	0	2	67	2	100	1	33
Total Respondents	16		4		5		3		2		3	
9. The Chief Purchasing Officer												
A. *Title*												
(1) Purchasing Agent	0	0	0	0	0	0	0	0	1	33	0	0
(2) Manager of Purchasing	3	9	0	0	0	0	0	0	0	0	0	0
(3) Director of Purchasing	15	47	4	80	3	50	1	33	1	33	3	100
(4) VP of Purchasing	11	34	1	20	2	33	2	67	0	0	0	0
(5) Materials Manager	0	0	0	0	0	0	0	0	0	0	0	0
(6) Director of Purchasing	0	0	0	0	1	17	0	0	0	0	0	0
(7) VP of Materials Management	2	6	0	0	0	0	0	0	0	0	0	0
(8) Other	1	3	0	0	0	0	1	33	1	33	0	0
Total Respondents	32	99%	5	100%	6	100%	3	100%	3	99%	3	100%
B. *Age*												
(1) 30-40	3	10	0	0	2	33	1	33	1	33	1	33
(2) 41-50	13	42	2	40	3	50	1	33	1	33	1	33
(3) 51-60	14	45	3	60	0	0	1	33	1	33	1	33
(4) Over 60	1	3	0	0	1	17	0	0	0	0	0	0
Total Respondents	31	100%	5	100%	6	100%	3	99%	3	99%	3	99%
Average age:	50		52		46		46		46		43	
C. *Education*												
(1) High school	1	3	0	0	0	0	0	0	0	0	2	67
(2) Bachelor's degree	16	52	2	40	5	83	3	100	1	33	1	33
(3) Graduate degree	14	45	3	60	1	17	0	0	2	67	0	0
Total Respondents	31	100%	5	100%	6	100%	3	100%	3	100%	3	100%
D. *Specialization in Bachelor's Degree*												
(1) Business	18	60	3	60	2	33	2	67	2	67	0	0
(2) Engineering	5	17	0	0	2	33	0	0	1	33	1	100
(3) Liberal Arts	2	7	0	0	2	33	1	33	0	0	0	0
(4) Other	5	17	2	40	0	0	0	0	0	0	0	0
Total Respondents	30	101%	5	100%	6	99%	3	100%	3	100%	1	100%
E. *Years in Present Position*												
(1) Under 1 year	2	6	0	0	0	0	0	0	0	0	0	0
(2) 1-5 years	15	47	2	40	5	83	1	33	3	100	1	33
(3) 6-10 years	7	22	1	20	1	17	1	33	0	0	1	33
(4) 11-15 years	6	19	2	40	0	0	0	0	0	0	1	33
(5) Over 15 years	2	6	0	0	0	0	1	33	0	0	0	0
Total Respondents	32	100%	5	100%	6	100%	3	99%	3	100%	3	99%
Average years in present position:	6		8		4		15		1		9	
F. *Years with present employer*												
(1) Under 1 year	1	3	0	0	0	0	0	0	0	0	0	0
(2) 1-5 years	6	19	0	0	1	17	1	33	0	0	0	0
(3) 6-10 years	6	19	1	20	1	17	0	0	3	100	0	0
(4) 11-15 years	3	9	0	0	2	33	0	0	0	0	1	33
(5) Over 15 years	16	50	4	30	2	33	2	67	0	0	2	67
Total Respondents	32	100%	5	100%	6	100%	3	100%	3	100%	3	100%
Average years with present employer:	17		22		16		21		9		27	
G. *Average years experience in all functional areas*												
(1) Purchasing		18		21		5		4		.7		17
(2) Operations/production		3		4		7		19		8		13
(3) Engineering		1		0		.2		0		2		3
(4) Marketing		.5		.8		0		0		9		0
(5) Finance		.6		0		0		0		0		0
(6) MIS		.3		0		8		0		0		0
(7) Traffic		.2		0		.5		0		1		6
(8) Accounting		.3		0		0		0		0		0
(9) Other		1		1		2.5		0		0		0
Total Respondents		31		5		6		3		3		3

ORGANIZATIONAL RELATIONSHIP DATA BY INDUSTRY

Sections 1–5

INDUSTRY	Paper No.	Paper %	Printing & Publishing No.	P&P %	Chemicals No.	Chem %	Petroleum & Coal No.	Pet %	Rubber & Plastics No.	R&P %	Stone, Clay, Glass No.	SCG %
1. Responding Organizations, 1986 $ Sales												
A. Less than $500 million	2	29	3	43	6	19	1	5	4	40	1	20
B. $500 million to 1 billion	1	14	2	29	5	16	1	5	1	10	0	0
C. $1.1 billion to 5 billion	3	43	2	29	15	47	7	32	4	40	4	80
D. $5.1 billion to 10 billion	1	14	0	0	4	13	3	14	1	10	0	0
E. Over $10 billion	0	0	0	0	2	6	10	45	0	0	0	0
Total Respondents	7	100%	7	101%	32	101%	22	101%	10	100%	5	100%
2. Number of Professional Purchasing Personnel												
A. 25 or less	4	57	6	86	12	39	8	36	7	70	1	20
B. 26 to 100	2	29	1	14	11	35	9	41	2	20	2	40
C. 101 to 250	1	14	0	0	4	13	2	9	1	10	2	40
D. 251 to 500	0	0	0	0	3	10	2	9	0	0	0	0
E. 501 to 1,000	0	0	0	0	1	3	1	5	0	0	0	0
F. 1,001 and over	0	0	0	0	0	0	0	0	0	0	0	0
Total Respondents	7	100%	7	100%	31	100%	22	100%	10	100%	5	100%
Average number of purchasing professionals:	47		18		124		97		41		70	
3. Organizational Structure												
A. Centralized	3	43	2	29	5	16	4	18	4	40	0	0
B. Centralized/Decentralized	3	43	5	71	26	81	17	77	5	50	4	80
C. Decentralized	1	14	0	0	1	3	1	5	1	10	1	20
Total Responding	7	100%	7	100%	32	100%	22	100%	10	100%	5	100%
4. Reporting Relationships of Purchasing — Purchasing reports to:												
A. President	0	0	0	0	4	13	2	9	3	30	0	0
B. Executive VP	2	29	2	29	6	19	4	18	3	30	2	40
C. Financial VP	0	0	1	14	3	9	4	18	0	0	1	20
D. Mfg./Opers./Prod. VP	3	43	2	29	7	22	3	14	2	20	0	0
E. Materials Mgmt. VP	0	0	0	0	3	9	1	5	0	0	0	0
F. Engineering VP	0	0	0	0	0	0	0	0	0	0	0	0
G. Administrative VP	2	29	2	29	6	19	6	27	0	0	0	0
H. Other	0	0	0	0	3	9	1	5	2	20	2	40
Total Respondents	7	101%	7	101%	32	101%	22	101%	10	100%	5	100%
5. Functions Reporting to Purchasing												
A. Inbound traffic only	1	14%	0	0%	2	6%	2	9%	1	10%	1	20%
B. Outbound traffic only	0	0	0	0	1	3	0	0	0	0	0	0
C. Inbound and outbound traffic	1	14	1	14	8	25	9	41	3	30	3	60
D. Warehousing and stores	5	71	3	43	8	25	10	45	5	50	2	40
E. Inventory control	5	71	3	43	9	28	13	59	9	90	2	40
F. Scrap/surplus disposal	3	43	5	71	17	53	18	82	7	70	3	60
G. Receiving	0	0	4	57	5	16	6	27	3	30	1	20
H. Incoming inspection	0	0	3	43	3	9	9	41	0	0	1	20
I. Other	1	14	0	0	9	28	5	23	2	20	1	20
Total Respondents	7	101%	7	101%	32	101%	21		10		5	

6. Activity Areas Newly Assigned to Purchasing and Activity Areas in Which Purchasing Has Assumed an Increased Role/Responsibility (Since 1980).

	Paper NA No.	Paper NA %	Paper IR No.	Paper IR %	P&P NA No.	P&P NA %	P&P IR No.	P&P IR %	Chem NA No.	Chem NA %	Chem IR No.	Chem IR %	Pet NA No.	Pet NA %	Pet IR No.	Pet IR %	R&P NA No.	R&P NA %	R&P IR No.	R&P IR %	SCG NA No.	SCG NA %	SCG IR No.	SCG IR %
A. Strategic planning	0	0	5	71	1	17	3	50	0	0	17	53	1	5	6	29	0	0	4	40	0	0	0	0
B. Product development	1	14	3	43	0	0	2	33	0	0	13	41	0	0	4	19	0	0	1	10	0	0	1	20
C. Traffic/transportation	0	0	4	57	1	17	0	0	3	9	11	34	3	14	5	24	0	0	1	10	3	60	0	0
D. New product evaluation	0	0	1	14	0	0	2	33	1	3	9	28	0	0	4	19	1	10	2	20	1	20	2	40
E. Capital equipment buys	0	0	4	57	1	17	3	50	4	13	17	53	0	0	5	24	0	0	1	10	0	0	0	0
F. Personnel travel	0	0	0	0	1	17	3	50	4	13	6	19	3	14	4	19	1	10	0	0	0	0	0	0
G. Marketing planning	0	0	2	29	0	0	1	17	0	0	7	22	0	0	4	19	0	0	1	10	0	0	2	40
H. Providing economic forecasts/indicators	0	0	6	86	1	17	4	67	2	6	16	50	0	0	10	48	1	10	5	50	0	0	0	0
I. Commodity futures trading	0	0	0	0	0	0	0	0	1	3	3	9	1	5	0	0	0	0	2	20	0	0	2	40
J. Cash-flow planning	0	0	2	29	0	0	0	0	4	13	5	16	1	5	2	20	0	0	2	20	0	0	1	20
K. Countertrade/offset planning/execution	0	0	2	29	0	0	0	0	4	13	8	25	1	5	2	20	0	0	2	20	0	0	1	20

A. Use materials management
B. Don't use materials management
Total Respondents

	(1) n	%	(2) n	%	(3) n	%	(4) n	%	(5) n	%	(6) n	%
A. Use materials management	5	71	1	20	23	72	13	59	8	80	1	20
B. Don't use materials management	2	29	4	80	9	28	9	41	2	20	4	80
Total Respondents	7	100%	5	100%	32	100%	22	100%	10	100%	5	100%

8. Functions Included Under the Materials Manager, in the Organizations Using Materials Management:

	(1) n	%	(2) n	%	(3) n	%	(4) n	%	(5) n	%	(6) n	%
A. Purchasing	5	100%	1	100%	19	83%	10	77%	7	88%	1	100%
B. Inventory	5	100	1	100	19	83	13	100	5	63	1	100
C. Production scheduling and control	3	60	1	100	19	83	1	8	5	63	1	100
D. Inbound traffic	4	80	1	100	20	87	6	46	5	63	1	100
E. Warehousing and stores	5	100	1	100	21	91	12	92	5	63	0	0
F. Incoming quality control	0	0	1	100	1	4	8	62	8	62	0	0
Total Respondents	5		1		23		13		8		1	

9. The Chief Purchasing Officer

A. *Title*

	(1) n	%	(2) n	%	(3) n	%	(4) n	%	(5) n	%	(6) n	%
(1) Purchasing Agent	0	0	0	0	0	0	0	0	0	0	0	0
(2) Manager of Purchasing	0	14	1	14	2	6	12	55	2	20	0	0
(3) Director of Purchasing	4	57	4	57	16	50	3	14	3	30	1	20
(4) VP of Purchasing	2	29	1	14	10	31	2	9	3	30	4	80
(5) Materials Manager	1	14	0	0	0	0	1	5	0	0	0	0
(6) Director of Purchasing	0	0	1	14	0	0	1	5	0	0	0	0
(7) VP of Materials Management	0	0	0	0	2	6	1	5	2	20	0	0
(8) Other	0	0	0	0	2	6	2	9	0	0	0	0
Total Respondents	7	100%	7	99%	32	99%	22	102%	10	100%	5	100%

B. *Age*

	(1) n	%	(2) n	%	(3) n	%	(4) n	%	(5) n	%	(6) n	%
(1) 30-40	0	0	1	14	3	9	2	9	2	20	2	40
(2) 41-50	3	43	3	43	10	31	12	55	1	10	2	40
(3) 51-60	3	43	2	29	17	53	8	36	7	70	1	20
(4) Over 60	1	14	1	14	2	6	0	0	0	0	0	0
Total Respondents	7	100%	7	100%	32	99%	22	100%	10	100%	5	100%
Average age:	50		48		51		48		52		46	

C. *Education*

	(1) n	%	(2) n	%	(3) n	%	(4) n	%	(5) n	%	(6) n	%
(1) High school	1	14	1	14	1	3	1	5	1	10	0	0
(2) Bachelor's degree	3	43	4	57	15	47	12	55	5	50	1	20
(3) Graduate degree	3	43	2	29	16	50	9	41	4	40	4	80
Total Respondents	7	100%	7	100%	32	100%	22	101%	10	100%	5	100%

D. *Specialization in Bachelor's Degree*

	(1) n	%	(2) n	%	(3) n	%	(4) n	%	(5) n	%	(6) n	%
(1) Business	4	67	5	83	10	33	10	48	3	38	1	20
(2) Engineering	1	17	0	0	10	33	6	29	2	25	2	40
(3) Liberal Arts	0	0	1	17	5	17	1	5	1	13	1	20
(4) Other	1	17	0	0	5	17	4	19	2	25	1	20
Total Respondents	6	101%	6	100%	30	100%	21	101%	8	101%	5	100%

E. *Years in Present Position*

	(1) n	%	(2) n	%	(3) n	%	(4) n	%	(5) n	%	(6) n	%
(1) Under 1 year	0	0	0	0	0	0	0	0	0	0	0	0
(2) 1-5 years	4	57	3	43	20	63	16	73	5	50	5	100
(3) 6-10 years	2	29	2	29	4	13	3	14	2	20	0	0
(4) 11-15 years	1	14	1	14	6	19	2	9	1	10	0	0
(5) Over 15 years	0	0	1	14	2	6	1	5	2	20	0	0
Total Respondents	7	100%	7	100%	32	101%	22	101%	10	100%	5	100%
Average years in present position:	5		8		6		5		8		2	

F. *Years with present employer*

	(1) n	%	(2) n	%	(3) n	%	(4) n	%	(5) n	%	(6) n	%
(1) Under 1 year	0	0	0	0	0	0	0	0	0	0	0	0
(2) 1-5 years	1	14	0	0	3	9	1	5	0	0	0	0
(3) 6-10 years	1	14	1	14	1	3	4	18	2	20	2	40
(4) 11-15 years	1	14	3	43	7	22	1	5	0	0	0	0
(5) Over 15 years	4	57	3	43	21	66	16	73	8	80	3	60
Total Respondents	7	99%	7	100%	32	101%	22	101%	10	100%	5	100%
Average years with present employer:	18		17		23		21		27		20	

G. *Average years experience in all functional areas*

	(1)	(2)	(3)	(4)	(5)	(6)
(1) Purchasing	19	19	15	14	13	2.6
(2) Operations/production	2.5	1	4	4	5	4
(3) Engineering	.7	.7	1.6	1.8	2	.8
(4) Marketing	.9	2.7	.6	.3	1	.6
(5) Finance	3.0	.4	.4	.1	2	.4
(6) MIS	.3	1.7	.4	.2	3	.0
(7) Traffic	.1	.0	.3	.7	4	3
(8) Accounting	.0	.0	.9	.3	0	0
(9) Other	7	7	.9	.3	0	5
Total Respondents	7	17	32	22	10	20

ORGANIZATIONAL RELATIONSHIP DATA BY INDUSTRY

Questions 1–5

INDUSTRY	Primary Metals No.	%	Fabricated Metal Products No.	%	Machinery, Except Electrical No.	%	Electric, Electronic Equipment No.	%	Transportation Equipment No.	%	Instruments, Related Products No.	%
1. Responding Organizations, 1986 $ Sales												
A. Less than $500 million	3	20	4	44	9	64	10	25	3	25	3	60
B. $500 million to 1 billion	2	13	2	22	3	21	8	20	2	17	1	20
C. $1.1 billion to 5 billion	9	60	2	22	2	14	13	33	5	42	1	20
D. $5.1 billion to 10 billion	1	7	0	0	0	0	6	15	1	8	0	0
E. Over $10 billion	0	0	1	11	0	0	3	8	1	8	0	0
Total Respondents	15	100%	9	99%	14	99%	40	101%	12	100%	5	100%
2. Number of Professional Purchasing Personnel												
A. 25 or less	6	40	4	44	12	86	13	33	3	25	3	60
B. 26 to 100	9	60	1	11	0	0	9	23	4	33	1	20
C. 101 to 250	0	0	3	33	1	7	9	23	1	8	1	20
D. 251 to 500	0	0	0	0	1	7	4	10	2	17	0	0
E. 501 to 1,000	0	0	0	0	0	0	2	5	1	8	0	0
F. 1,001 and over	0	0	1	11	0	0	2	5	1	8	0	0
Total Respondents	15	100%	9	99%	14	100%	39	99%	12	99%	5	100%
Average number of purchasing professionals:	40		138		43		233		269		34	
3. Organizational Structure												
A. Centralized	3	20	2	22	3	21	8	20	2	17	3	60
B. Centralized/Decentralized	11	73	2	22	6	43	25	63	7	58	1	20
C. Decentralized	1	7	5	56	5	36	7	18	3	25	1	20
Total Responding	15	100%	9	100%	14	100%	40	101%	12	100%	5	100%
4. Reporting Relationships of Purchasing — Purchasing reports to:												
A. President	4	31	3	33	1	7	6	15	1	8	0	0
B. Executive VP	2	15	3	33	1	7	5	13	2	17	0	0
C. Financial VP	1	8	0	0	0	0	3	8	0	0	0	0
D. Mfg./Opers./Prod. VP	0	0	0	0	6	43	14	36	5	42	1	20
E. Materials Mgmt. VP	2	15	0	0	1	7	4	10	1	8	2	40
F. Engineering VP	0	0	0	0	0	0	0	0	0	0	0	0
G. Administrative VP	3	23	1	11	2	14	1	3	1	8	1	20
H. Other	1	8	2	22	3	21	6	15	2	17	1	20
Total Respondents	13	100%	9	99%	14	99%	39	100%	12	100%	5	100%
5. Functions Reporting to Purchasing												
A. Inbound traffic only	0	0%	0	0%	1	7%	4	10%	1	8%	0	0%
B. Outbound traffic only	0	0	0	0	0	0	0	0	0	0	0	0
C. Inbound and outbound traffic	6	40	6	67	6	43	12	30	5	42	1	20
D. Warehousing and stores	5	33	3	33	4	29	9	23	1	8	0	0
E. Inventory control	6	40	3	33	9	64	10	25	5	42	2	40
F. Scrap/surplus disposal	13	87	4	44	9	64	17	43	5	42	2	40
G. Receiving	3	20	1	11	2	14	10	25	1	8	0	0
H. Incoming inspection	3	20	1	11	0	0	7	18	2	17	1	20
I. Other	1	7	5	56	8	57	6	15	6	50	1	20
Total Respondents	15		9		14		40		12		5	

6. Activity Areas Newly Assigned to Purchasing and Activity Areas in Which Purchasing Has Assumed an Increased Role/Responsibility (Since 1980).

	Primary Metals Newly No.	%	Increased No.	%	Fabricated Metal Products Newly No.	%	Increased No.	%	Machinery, Except Electrical Newly No.	%	Increased No.	%	Electric, Electronic Equipment Newly No.	%	Increased No.	%	Transportation Equipment Newly No.	%	Increased No.	%	Instruments, Related Products Newly No.	%	Increased No.	%
A. Strategic planning	2	14	5	36	1	11	5	56	4	29	4	29	7	18	19	48	0	0	8	67	0	0	0	0
B. Product development	0	0	2	14	1	11	2	22	1	7	3	21	5	13	11	28	0	0	6	50	0	0	1	20
C. Traffic/transportation	3	21	4	29	3	33	2	22	3	21	3	21	5	13	7	18	1	8	2	17	0	0	3	60
D. New product evaluation	1	7	5	36	1	11	3	33	4	29	1	7	3	7	7	18	0	0	6	50	0	0	1	20
E. Capital equipment buys	1	7	5	36	1	11	2	22	3	21	2	14	8	20	17	43	1	8	4	33	0	0	1	20
F. Personnel travel	2	14	2	14	0	0	1	11	2	14	2	14	2	5	7	18	0	0	0	0	2	40	1	20
G. Marketing planning	0	0	1	7	0	0	1	11	1	7	2	14	1	3	7	18	1	8	6	50	2	40	0	0
H. Providing economic forecasts/indicators	0	0	7	50	0	0	4	44	3	21	3	21	5	13	15	38	0	0	6	50	0	0	1	20
I. Commodity futures trading	0	0	1	7	0	0	1	11	0	0	1	7	3	8	3	8	0	0	1	8	0	0	0	0
J. Cash-flow planning	0	0	3	21	2	22	1	11	1	7	0	0	3	8	2	5	0	0	1	8	0	0	1	20
K. Countertrade/offset planning/execution	4	29	4	29	3	33	2	22	1	7	3	21	6	15	9	23	0	0	5	42	1	20	0	0
Total Respondents	14		14		9		9		14		14		40				12				5			

7. Materials Management Concepts
8. Functions Included Under the Materials Manager, in the Organizations Using Materials Management:
9. The Chief Purchasing Officer

	Col 1 (N)	Col 1 (%)	Col 2 (N)	Col 2 (%)	Col 3 (N)	Col 3 (%)	Col 4 (N)	Col 4 (%)	Col 5 (N)	Col 5 (%)	Col 6 (N)	Col 6 (%)
7. Materials Management Concepts												
A. Use materials management	3	60	11	92	29	73	13	93	7	78	9	64
B. Don't use materials management	2	40	1	8	11	28	1	7	2	22	5	36
Total Respondents	5	100%	12	100%	40	101%	14	100%	9	100%	14	101%
8. Functions Included Under the Materials Manager:												
A. Purchasing	3	100%	10	91%	29	100%	10	77%	5	71%	8	89%
B. Inventory	3	100	10	91	28	97	12	92	7	100	8	89
C. Production scheduling and control	3	100	8	73	22	76	11	85	7	100	4	44
D. Inbound traffic	2	67	8	73	24	83	11	85	3	43	6	67
E. Warehousing and stores	2	67	7	64	24	83	13	100	7	100	7	78
F. Incoming quality control	0	0	0	0	12	41	3	23	2	29	3	33
Total Respondents	3		11		29		13		7		9	
9. The Chief Purchasing Officer												
A. Title												
(1) Purchasing Agent	0	0	0	0	0	0	0	0	0	0	0	0
(2) Manager of Purchasing	2	40	4	33	8	20	3	21	1	11	1	7
(3) Director of Purchasing	1	20	4	33	12	30	7	50	3	33	8	53
(4) VP of Purchasing	0	0	2	17	7	18	1	7	2	22	4	27
(5) Materials Manager	0	0	0	0	1	3	2	14	0	0	0	0
(6) Director of Purchasing	0	0	0	0	7	18	0	0	0	0	1	7
(7) VP of Materials Management	0	0	1	8	4	10	1	7	2	22	0	0
(8) Other	2	40	1	8	1	3	0	0	1	11	1	7
Total Respondents	5	100%	12	99%	40	102%	14	99%	9	99%	15	101%
B. Age												
(1) 30-40	1	25	3	27	5	13	3	21	1	13	2	15
(2) 41-50	2	50	3	27	18	45	6	43	4	50	1	8
(3) 51-60	1	25	3	27	13	33	5	36	1	13	9	69
(4) Over 60	0	0	2	18	4	10	0	0	2	25	1	8
Total Respondents	4	100%	11	99%	40	101%	14	100%	8	101%	13	100%
Average age:	48		49		50		47		49		52	
C. Education												
(1) High school	0	0	1	8	2	5	0	0	0	0	2	14
(2) Bachelor's degree	4	80	6	50	27	68	11	79	5	56	6	43
(3) Graduate degree	1	20	5	42	11	28	3	21	4	44	6	43
Total Respondents	5	100%	12	100%	40	101%	14	100%	9	100%	14	100%
D. Specialization in Bachelor's Degree												
(1) Business	2	50	8	73	20	56	7	50	5	63	6	50
(2) Engineering	0	0	1	9	6	17	2	14	1	13	4	33
(3) Liberal Arts	1	25	1	9	7	19	1	7	1	13	2	17
(4) Other	1	25	1	9	3	8	4	29	1	13	0	0
Total Respondents	4	100%	11	100%	36	100%	14	100%	8	102%	12	100%
E. Years in Present Position												
(1) Under 1 year	0	0	0	0	1	3	0	0	0	0	0	0
(2) 1-5 years	3	60	5	42	21	54	8	57	4	44	9	60
(3) 6-10 years	1	20	7	58	8	21	5	36	1	11	5	33
(4) 11-15 years	1	20	0	0	4	10	0	0	2	22	1	7
(5) Over 15 years	0	0	0	0	5	13	1	7	2	22	0	0
Total Respondents	5	100%	12	100%	39	101%	14	100%	9	99%	15	100%
Average years in present position:	5		6		7		6		9		6	
F. Years with present employer												
(1) Under 1 year	0	0	0	0	0	0	0	0	0	0	0	0
(2) 1-5 years	1	20	0	0	5	13	3	21	3	33	1	7
(3) 6-10 years	1	20	2	17	13	33	2	14	0	0	1	7
(4) 11-15 years	0	0	3	25	2	5	3	21	2	22	1	7
(5) Over 15 years	3	60	7	58	20	50	6	43	4	44	12	80
Total Respondents	5	100%	12	100%	40	101%	14	99%	9	99%	15	101%
Average years with present employer:	13		20		16		13		17		24	
G. Average years experience in all functional areas												
(1) Purchasing	21		19		16		17		19		22	
(2) Operations/production	2		2		5		3		1		1	
(3) Engineering	0		.6		1		.5		.5		0	
(4) Marketing	0		.5		2		1.6		.3		1.5	
(5) Finance	0		1.6		.6		.3		.0		.7	
(6) MIS	0		.8		1.4		.8		.9		.2	
(7) Traffic	2		2.5		1		.2		.2		0	
(8) Accounting	0		.6		1		.0		.0		0	
(9) Other	4		.2									
Total Respondents	5		12		40		14		9		15	

ORGANIZATIONAL RELATIONSHIP DATA BY INDUSTRY

INDUSTRY

Sections 1–5

	Miscellaneous Manufacturing No.	%	Aerospace No.	%	Retail/Trade/Distribution No.	%	Government (Nonprofit) No.	%	Service No.	%
1. Responding Organizations, 1986 $ Sales										
A. Less than $500 million	10	71	3	17	0	0	3	75	5	17
B. $500 million to 1 billion	1	7	3	17	0	0	1	25	3	10
C. $1.1 billion to 5 billion	2	14	5	28	1	50	0	0	16	55
D. $5.1 billion to 10 billion	0	0	4	22	0	0	0	0	3	10
E. Over $10 billion	1	7	3	17	1	50	0	0	2	7
Total Respondents	14	99%	18	101%	2	100%	4	100%	29	99%
2. Number of Professional Purchasing Personnel										
A. 25 or less	10	77	2	11	1	100	2	50	17	59
B. 26 to 100	2	15	4	22	0	0	2	50	9	31
C. 101 to 250	0	0	4	22	0	0	0	0	1	3
D. 251 to 500	1	8	3	17	0	0	0	0	1	3
E. 501 to 1,000	0	0	3	17	0	0	0	0	1	3
F. 1,001 and over	0	0	2	11	0	0	0	0	0	0
Total Respondents	13	100%	18	100%	1	100%	4	100%	29	99%
Average number of purchasing professionals:	54		421		12		36		64	
3. Organizational Structure										
A. Centralized	2	14	3	17	1	50	3	75	10	36
B. Centralized/Decentralized	6	43	11	61	1	50	1	25	17	61
C. Decentralized	6	43	4	22	0	0	0	0	1	4
Total Respondents	14	100%	18	100%	2	100%	4	100%	28	101%
4. Reporting Relationships of Purchasing Purchasing reports to:										
A. President	2	14	3	18	1	50	0	0	7	24
B. Executive VP	1	7	4	24	1	50	0	0	6	21
C. Financial VP	3	21	0	0	0	0	1	25	3	10
D. Mfg./Opers./Prod. VP	2	14	6	35	0	0	0	0	6	21
E. Materials Mgmt. VP	1	7	1	6	0	0	0	0	1	3
F. Engineering VP	0	0	0	0	0	0	0	0	1	3
G. Administrative VP	2	14	2	12	0	0	1	25	5	17
H. Other	3	21	1	6	1	50	2	50	0	0
Total Respondents	14	98%	17	101%	2	100%	4	100%	29	99%
5. Functions Reporting to Purchasing										
A. Inbound traffic only	3	21	1	6%	1	50%	0	0	3	10%
B. Outbound traffic only	0	0	0	0	0	0	0	0	1	3
C. Inbound and outbound traffic	2	14	7	39	0	0	2	50	13	45
D. Warehousing and stores	4	29	6	33	0	0	2	50	18	62
E. Inventory control	4	29	7	39	0	0	2	25	16	55
F. Scrap/surplus disposal	13	93	6	33	1	50	1	25	18	62
G. Receiving	4	29	5	28	0	0	1	25	15	52
H. Incoming inspection	1	7	1	6	0	0	0	0	8	28
I. Other	2	14	7	39	0	0	3	75	8	28
Total Respondents	14		18		2		4		29	

6. Activity Areas Newly Assigned to Purchasing and Activity Areas in Which Purchasing Has Assumed an Increased Role/Responsibility (Since 1980).

	Misc. Mfg. Newly Assigned No.	%	Increased Role/Resp. No.	%	Aerospace Newly Assigned No.	%	Increased Role/Resp. No.	%	Retail Newly Assigned No.	%	Increased Role/Resp. No.	%	Gov't Newly Assigned No.	%	Increased Role/Resp. No.	%	Service Newly Assigned No.	%	Increased Role/Resp. No.	%
A. Strategic planning	2	14	2	14	3	17	9	50	0	0	0	0	0	0	2	67	0	0	11	38
B. Product development	1	7	4	29	1	6	5	36	0	0	0	0	1	33	0	0	2	7	5	17
C. Traffic/transportation	0	0	0	0	0	0	1	6	1	50	0	0	0	0	1	33	5	17	10	34
D. New product evaluation	3	21	7	50	0	0	1	6	1	50	0	0	0	0	0	0	1	3	12	41
E. Capital equipment buys	1	7	1	7	3	17	7	39	0	0	0	0	1	33	2	67	2	7	13	45
F. Personnel travel	0	0	3	21	0	0	2	11	1	50	1	50	1	33	2	67	6	21	6	21
G. Marketing planning	0	0	5	36	0	0	1	6	0	0	0	0	0	0	0	0	2	7	9	31
H. Providing economic forecasts/indicators	0	0	3	21	0	0	2	11	0	0	0	0	0	0	1	33	3	10	9	31
I. Commodity futures trading	0	0	3	21	1	6	4	22	0	0	1	50	0	0	0	0	5	17	2	7
J. Cash-flow planning	0	0	8	57	6	33	5	27	0	0	1	50	0	0	1	33	4	14	6	21
K. Countertrade/offset planning/execution	1	7	9	64					0	0	0	0			0	0			0	0
Total Respondents	14		14		18		18		2		2		4		4					

7. Materials Management Concepts										
A. Use materials management	6	43	18	100	0	0	3	75	21	75
B. Don't use materials management	8	57	0	0	1	100	1	25	7	25
Total Respondents	14	100%	18	100%	1	100%	4	100%	28	100%
8. Functions Included Under the Materials Manager, in the Organizations Using Materials Management:										
A. Purchasing	6	100%	14	78%	0	0%	2	67%	18	86%
B. Inventory	6	100	16	89	0	0	3	100	21	100
C. Production scheduling and control	4	67	9	50	0	0	0	0	7	33
D. Inbound traffic	3	50	12	67	0	0	3	100	13	62
E. Warehousing and stores	6	100	12	67	0	0	3	100	20	95
F. Incoming quality control	1	17	1	6	0	0	0	0	10	48
Total Respondents	6		18		0		3		21	
9. The Chief Purchasing Officer										
A. *Title*										
(1) Purchasing Agent	0	0	0	0	0	0	0	0	1	3
(2) Manager of Purchasing	5	36	4	22	0	0	3	75	1	3
(3) Director of Purchasing	6	43	1	6	1	50	1	25	10	34
(4) VP of Purchasing	1	7	2	11	1	50	0	0	9	31
(5) Materials Manager	1	7	0	0	0	0	0	0	0	0
(6) Director of Purchasing	0	0	3	17	0	0	0	0	2	7
(7) VP of Materials Management	0	0	7	39	0	0	0	0	4	14
(8) Other	1	7	1	6	0	0	2	50	2	7
Total Respondents	14	100%	18	101%	2	100%	4	100%	29	99%
B. *Age*										
(1) 30-40	4	29	2	11	1	50	0	0	6	22
(2) 41-50	5	36	8	44	1	50	1	25	8	30
(3) 51-60	4	29	5	28	0	0	3	75	12	44
(4) Over 60	1	7	3	17	0	0	0	0	1	4
Total Respondents	14	101%	18	100%	2	100%	4	100%	27	100%
Average age:	48		50		41		53		49	
C. *Education*										
(1) High school	2	14	2	11	0	0	0	0	2	7
(2) Bachelor's degree	10	71	8	44	1	50	2	50	13	45
(3) Graduate degree	2	14	8	44	1	50	2	50	14	48
Total Respondents	14	99%	18	99%	2	100%	4	100%	29	100%
D. *Specialization in Bachelor's Degree*										
(1) Business	6	55	11	73	2	100	3	75	17	68
(2) Engineering	2	18	2	13	0	0	0	0	2	8
(3) Liberal Arts	3	27	1	7	0	0	0	0	3	12
(4) Other	0	0	1	7	0	0	1	25	3	12
Total Respondents	11	100%	15	100%	2	100%	4	100%	25	100%
E. *Years in Present Position*										
(1) Under 1 year	0	0	1	6	0	0	0	0	2	7
(2) 1-5 years	8	57	14	78	2	100	2	50	14	48
(3) 6-10 years	5	36	2	11	0	0	1	25	8	28
(4) 11-15 years	0	0	1	6	0	0	0	0	4	14
(5) Over 15 years	1	7	0	0	0	0	1	25	1	3
Total Respondents	14	100%	18	101%	2	100%	4	100%	29	100%
Average years in present position:	6		8		3		9		7	
F. *Years with present employer*										
(1) Under 1 year	0	0	0	0	0	0	0	0	1	3
(2) 1-5 years	2	14	3	17	1	50	0	0	3	10
(3) 6-10 years	3	21	4	22	0	0	2	50	8	28
(4) 11-15 years	2	14	2	11	0	0	0	0	5	17
(5) Over 15 years	7	50	9	50	1	50	2	50	12	41
Total Respondents	14	99%	18	100%	2	100%	4	100%	29	99%
Average years with present employer:	15		17		12		16		14	
G. *Average years experience in all functional areas*										
(1) Purchasing		20		19		7		27		15
(2) Operations/production		2		5		10		0		4.6
(3) Engineering		1.4		.8		0		0		1.8
(4) Marketing		.6		.8		0		0		1
(5) Finance		0		.7		0		0		.3
(6) MIS		.2		.1		0		0		0
(7) Traffic		0		2		3.5		0		0
(8) Accounting		0		C		0		0		.2
(9) Other		1		C		0		0		.5
Total Respondents		14		18		2		4		28

THE CENTER FOR ADVANCED PURCHASING STUDIES •

THE CENTER FOR ADVANCED PURCHASING STUDIES (CAPS) was established in November 1986 as a national affiliation agreement between the College of Business at Arizona State University and the National Association of Purchasing Management. It is located at The Arizona State University Research Park, 2055 East Centennial Circle, P.O. Box 22160, Tempe, AZ 85282-0960 (Telephone [602] 752-2277).

The Center has three major goals to be accomplished through its research program:

- to improve purchasing effectiveness and efficiency
- to improve overall purchasing capability
- to increase the competitiveness of U.S. companies in a global economy

Current research underway includes a Comparative Study of the Purchasing Process in the Service, Government, Institutional, Retail/Trade, and Industrial Sectors; Purchasing Ethical Practices; Global Purchasing; and World Class Purchasing Organizations and Practices.

CAPS, a 501 (c)(3) not-for-profit research organization is funded solely by tax-deductible contributions from corporations and individuals who want to make a difference in the state of purchasing and materials management knowledge. Policy guidance is provided by the Board of Trustees consisting of:

R. Jerry Baker, The National Association of Purchasing Management
Montague E. Cooper, Chevron U.S.A., Inc.
George Harris, TRW, Inc.
John H. Hoagland, Michigan State University
Stanley N. Sherman, George Washington University, and
Rene A. Yates, B.A. Ballou & Company, Inc., and the National Association of Purchasing Management

The Center for Advanced Purchasing Studies and the National Association of Purchasing Management wishes to thank the following corporations, foundations, and affiliated purchasing management associations for their financial support during 1987:

Americhem Inc.
Ameritech Services
ARCO
Avery, Materials Group
Barnes Group Foundation
BP America
Carter Chemicals & Services, Inc.
Caterpillar Inc.
Chevron U.S.A., Inc.
C.M. Almy & Sons, Inc.
Coastal Savings Bank
Concord Realstate Corp.
Corning Glass Works
Dragon Products Co.

Eastman Kodak Company
Ernst & Whinney
Firestone Trust Fund
Freeway Corp.
G.E. Company, Contracting/Purchasing
G.E. Company, Corporate Sourcing
The Glidden Company
The HCA Foundation
Hughes Aircraft
Imperial Litho/Graphics, Inc.
Intel Corporation
International Minerals & Chemical Corporation
Keithley Instruments, Inc.
The Lincoln Electric Company
Lockheed Leadership Fund
Loctite Corporation
L-Tec Welding & Cutting Systems
North Canton Tool Company
Northern Telecom Inc.
Ohio Power Company
Parker Hannifin Corporation
Shamrock Hose & Fitting Company
Simmons Precision Product Inc.
Society Corporation
Southern Pacific Transportation Co.
Texas Instruments Incorporated
TRW Foundation
Union Pacific Railroad Co.
U.S. West Materiel Resources, Inc.

Purchasing Management Association of Canton
Purchasing Management Association of Cleveland
Purchasing Management Association of Denver
Purchasing Management Association of Detroit
Purchasing Management Association of Eastern Iowa
Purchasing Management Association of Florida First Coast
Purchasing Management Association of Florida Gold Coast
Purchasing Management Association of Georgia
Purchasing Management Association of Kansas City
The Lima Area Purchasing Management Association
Purchasing Management Association of New Jersey
Purchasing Management Association of New Mexico
Purchasing Management Association of Old Dominion, Inc.
Purchasing Management Association of Spokane
Purchasing Management Association of Western Michigan
Twin City Purchasing Management Association

CENTER FOR ADVANCED PURCHASING STUDIES
Arizona State University Research Park
2055 East Centennial Circle
P.O. Box 22160
Tempe, Arizona 85282
(602) 752-2277

ISBN   0-945968-00-0